issues 1968

iSSUeS 1968

NORMAN COUSINS

J. W. FULBRIGHT

ROBERT F. KENNEDY

MARTIN LUTHER KING, JR.

ALFRED M. LANDON

RALPH McGILL

RONALD REAGAN

GEORGE ROMNEY

Edited by WILLIAM W. BOYER
With a Foreword by JAMES A. McCAIN

THE UNIVERSITY PRESS OF KANSAS
Lawrence and London

Foreword

THE lectures comprising this volume were originally scheduled and delivered in order to achieve two objectives: in the case of the Alfred M. Landon Lectures, as a tribute to a distinguished Kansan and American, and, in the case of the entire series, to implement more effectively the vital role of the university as a free marketplace of ideas.

Alf Landon, of course, achieved distinction first as Governor of Kansas and then Republican Party nominee for the Presidency of the United States. However, it has been in more recent years in the role of elder statesman that he is giving his fullest measure of service to his state and nation. His periodic statements on the controversial and often emotionally overheated issues of our time have been widely reported in the American press and have been invariably wise, penetrating, and forthright. It is no wonder that the eminent Americans invited to honor him by serving as Landon Lecturers accepted the invitation so readily.

The university must be the implacable foe of what the *Saturday Review* once labeled "the mummification of opinion." Early in the last century Alexis de Tocqueville declared, "I know of no country in which there is so little independence of mind and real freedom of discussion as in America." And about a hundred years later Santayana found conditions little better, as evidenced by his complaint, "American life is a powerful solvent. . . . It seems to neutralize every intellectual element, however tough and alien it may be, and to fuse it in the native goodwill, complacency, thoughtlessness and optimism."

Nowhere is there better evidence that we no longer deserve such strictures than in the intellectual ferment on today's university campus and the militancy with which students advocate their political views.

The militants, of course, are a small minority. Significantly, the great rank and file of our students today display a depth of concern over the world off the campus absolutely without precedent in the history of American higher education. Hoping to exploit this concern and to cultivate for the years ahead a quality of citizenship commensurate with the awesome demands upon it, we have brought these speakers to the campus to supplement and reinforce the influence of formal instruction.

We are fortunate in the variety, importance, and timeliness of the issues covered in this volume and the authority with which these issues are discussed. It is our hope to share with the general public through this volume the wisdom and insights which these lectures brought to our campus.

JAMES A. McCAIN
President
Kansas State University.

Contents

issues 1968

The Age
of Acceleration

Norman Cousins

THERE was no problem, Hegel liked to think, that was not penetrable by thought. This is encouraging enough, but Hegel lived at a time when the problem of scrutinizing living history was not yet battered and confounded by acceleration. The trouble with trying to penetrate the vitals of the past quarter century is that 1940 was more than a hundred years ago. Into a few decades have been compressed more change, more thrust, more tossing about of men's souls and gizzards than had been spaced out over most of the human chronicle until then. The metabolism of history has gone berserk.

What is most significant, therefore, about the past twenty-five years is not the extent of change but the pace of change. A man's legs are forty times longer than they were a generation ago, measured by his increased speed and mobility. He has developed more potent energy during the past twenty-five years than during the previous twenty-five hundred years. And the rate of acceleration continues to increase, a specific reflection of the fact that the number of scientists now alive is larger than all the scientists in all the ages of man put together before 1920.

The acceleration has done more than to impair the faculty of human observation and comprehension. It has created a tendency toward disorientation. It has unhinged the sense of vital balance that enables a man to locate himself in time and place. In the centrifuge of the twentieth century man is whirling away from the center of his own being. The farther out he spins, the more blurred his view of himself, of what he might be, and of his relationship to the nameless faces in the crowd. The separation is not just between body and place; it is between mind and reason.

The connection between the acceleration and man's anxiety has been widely observed and documented. The same is true of computerization and its tendency to wash the color out of human personality. Less fully identified and scrutinized is the fact that ultimately the acceleration produces irreverence. Men in increasing motion cover ground but have none to stand on. Values take on a free-floating quality. The disconnection makes for distortion and an unfamiliarity that breeds contempt. It is not just a matter of rejecting values; it is a matter of being disconnected from the things that give rise to values. Obviously, not all irreverence is bad. The irreverence that challenges, that peels back the layers of sham, that releases bitterness or anger against attempts to cheapen life—this in itself is an assertion of values. But the main vein of irreverence in our time is quite different. It is nihilistic, brutal, anti-human. Basically, it is directed against life itself.

The symptoms are fundamental. They are not just a street mob goading a man on a ledge to take the plunge. Nor a crowd in a subway passively observing one man carving up another. Nor people paying for the privilege of seeing people get hurt. Nor rapacious comedians mistaking verbal brutality for wit. Irreverence in the twentieth century has a more pervasive accent. It involves the basic mood of large numbers of people and the kind of culture they are prepared to support. It is visible in the abrasiveness of human relations that many people either prefer or seem to take for granted.

These things haven't occurred because of some historical quirk. They are the product of specific gravity and direct cause. They reflect and are part of a dominant theme. The theme is the volcanic eruption of the scientific intelligence, throwing hot lava over the whole of man's estate, most especially over the national structures. A nation meant many things to an individual, but most of all it meant protection—protection against other tribes, protection against disorder from within. This protection, from without or within, required force. Then, suddenly, out of the acceleration came a new kind of force that changed everything about the state except its awareness that a fundamental change had come about. Man became deprived of his protection. The power was total, obliterative, suicidal. The feasibility of war became obsolete but the habit of war and the situations that produced war remained unchanged.

NORMAN COUSINS

The nations possessing nuclear weapons knew that any general use of atomic force could shatter the natural environment that made life possible. Yet each dreaded having the other think it lacked the nerve to go through with the apocalypse if it had to. And so each made unambiguous proclamations about its readiness to use all the power at its disposal in behalf of its vital interests. But the use of the power would expunge these vital interests, along with everything else. Thus the central need was to find some way of creating security which, when employed, would not be destructive of that security.

The ultimate effect, therefore, of the acceleration has been to make life tentative. Life that is tentative has a tendency to become cheap. What does it mean to live in an age when the defensive level of human beings has been reduced to that of insects against a blowtorch? The most enshrined phrase in the lexicon of philosophers is the dignity of man, yet dignity does not depend only on political charters or declarations. Dignity also means solidity; it means a moral contract accepting life as infinitely precious. How much reverence for life is possible when everyone knows that the flick of a finger can incinerate a billion human beings and that a nod can release tons of disease germs? A painful world man can train himself to endure, but a world that on the whim of a madman can become a crematorium or a disease chamber—this is the giant thief that steals a man's dignity and his reverence for life.

Man and his society are in a constant condition of interaction. At a time when nations can vaporize civilization, the individual takes on the temper of the total organism of which he is a part. He doesn't have to react on the level of conscious decision; he can reflect an environment that no longer fully comprehends the fragility and uniqueness of human life.

Any attack on the problem must begin not so much with a definition of acceleration as with a definition of man. If the theory of human perfectibility is rejected, then it may be only a matter of time before he becomes ground up in the wheels he has sent spinning so furiously. But if human uniqueness is defined as the capacity to conceive that which has never been conceived before, then acceleration can be relieved of its terrors. Man's difficulty has never been in doing things; it has been in choosing what to do. The ultimate test is not of skills but of purposes and desires. Man has already transformed nature; are we to say he is unable to transform himself? Is it reasonable to believe that a species that has demonstrated a capacity to lift itself off its planet is unable to raise its sights in devising a rational future? If awareness of the consequences of the present drift leads to a desire to avert them, the Age of Acceleration can lead to an Age of Balance.

Thomas Jefferson looked forward to a time when all barbarism would disappear from the earth. If he were alive today he would take note of the persistence and extension of barbarism but, as a believer in human perfectibility, he would warn against the conclusion that men are essentially barbarous. With Franklin, Emerson, William James, and Holmes, he would resist theories of historical inevitability. He would not be intimidated by the momentum of events into believing that a great reversal could not be brought about. He would also probably try to remind us that no idea figured more largely in the making of American society than that history was what men wanted it to be, and that civilization is what happens when men have intelligent desires. There is hope, then, in a plastic definition of man. This goes beyond the recognition of a divine itch or the sudden notion that there is an extra minute before midnight. Hope today—and it may be the only hope—resides in the world-wide emergence of the articulate and communicating citizen. What he wants and what he does mean more and more to the governments of which he is a part. The American experiment has succeeded in a way that Madison and Hamilton never dared dream it would. Its essential claim—that nothing is more important than man—has been echoed in every continent. The individual man has come into his own. Thinking, feeling, musing, complaining, fending, creating, building, evading, desiring, he has become more important to the operators of his governments than ever before. The question, therefore, is not whether man is capable of prolonging and ennobling his stay on earth. The question is whether he recognizes his prime power—and also his duty—for accomplishing that purpose.

What will cause Everyman, who lives everywhere, who is preoccupied with different things and who lives under different systems, suddenly to find both unison and resonance in calling for safety and sense on earth? Next, what is it he is expected to say? Finally, who will do the effective listening?

On the first question: Despite national boundaries and belligerently different ideological systems, the main confrontation in today's world cuts across national boundaries and ideological lines. The ultimate divisions take place within the societies, not between them. On one side are those who comprehend or sense the meaning of the acceleration, who perceive that new connections among men have to be created regardless of their diversity, and who move almost instinctively toward building those universal institutions that can serve the city of man. On the other side are those who think in terms of separatism, the perpetuation of group egos, the manning of tribal battle stations, and the lures of compartmentalization.

It is out of this transcendent confrontation that Everyman will make his voice and weight felt. He needs to be encouraged to believe that what he feels and wants to say can be part of a universal thrust. And it is here that writers, especially novelists, poets, and playwrights, have their finest opportunity. If we have learned nothing else, it is that the ideas of the poets and artists penetrate where everything else has failed. The question, therefore, is not so much whether Everyman is capable of response, whatever his station, as whether he has something and someone to respond to.

On the second question: It would be exhilarating, to say the least, if a shout were to go up all over the world for a human society under law. This is not likely to happen in the next twenty-four hours. All that is necessary to happen is the direct expression of raw concern. There is primitive, colossal energy in the simply stated but insistent call by enough people for a situation of reasonable safety on earth, for an end to anarchy in the dealings among states, and for easier access by members of the human family to one another.

On the third question: Even the most insulated and arbitrary government or system has to be concerned today about the turnings of the popular mind. Some systems may be less attuned than others but at some point all must pay attention.

The same acceleration that has produced disarray and irreverence can give man confidence in achieving big goals within the short time it is necessary to achieve them. It can give him confidence, too, in the reach of his intelligence for finding answers of almost infinite complexity. Progress lies not in a rejection of acceleration but in a proper respect for the possibilities of mind.

What Kind of a Country Do You Want America To Be?

J. W. Fulbright

Rіght at this moment there is little point in suggesting specific alternatives to the current American policy in Vietnam. This is not because an alternative is not needed—one has never been needed more. Nor is it because of an obligation to be silent in wartime; there is no such obligation—indeed, in a democracy a citizen has a clear obligation to speak out when he feels strongly that his government is embarked upon a disastrous course. The argument that dissent prolongs the war is unsound; even if the voices of dissent were to fall silent, the fact of a deeply divided America would still be apparent to North Vietnam from the newspaper columns and public opinion polls—unless of course these too were to be silenced. It is not the critics' dissent but the Administration's escalation that is prolonging the war and costing the lives of fine young Americans.

Being unwilling or unable to defend its war policy in rational debate, the Administration has resorted to the device of pretending that criticism of its war policy —which even *U. S. News and World Report* (May 8, 1967, p. 25) now calls a "flat failure"—is in reality an attack on America's fighting men in Vietnam. This is a calumny on our soldiers, whose burdens are heavy enough without the added burden of having to shield a bankrupt policy. A retired brigadier general of the United States Army, who served in both world wars and in the Korean War and who is ready to serve again, says nonetheless that "this does not release me from the duty, nor deny me the right of trying to keep my country on a prudent and enlightened course." And he adds, "Certainly the country is proud of General Westmoreland, and proud of the splendid forces which he commands. It does not follow that the country is obliged to send them, and itself to destruction" (Letter to the Editor from Brigadier General William Wallace Ford, *New York Times*, May 3, 1967, p. 44).

The Administration, however, is not interested in an alternative for Vietnam. It is deeply and, to all appearances, unalterably committed to its present course of military escalation. It has apparently staked its hopes for the 1968 election, its standing in history, and the lives of thousands of brave young Americans on the success of that policy. It was, I believe, for the double purpose of shielding that policy from criticism and of stirring up patriotic support for an expanded war that General Westmoreland was brought home to address a joint meeting of the Congress. Like a gambler who has had a long losing streak, the architects of the Vietnamese war postpone facing up to their failure by throwing good money after bad, by escalating the level of violence and sending more and more young Americans into the bitter and unnecessary battle.

Because they are so committed, beyond the reach of the democratic dialogue, there is little immediate purpose in reiterating detailed proposals for an alternative policy. Some of us in the Senate and many private citizens have tried to do exactly that; in my recent book, for example, I suggested eight specific steps that might be taken toward a settlement under which *neither* side would have to "turn tail and run." It has, I think, been clearly established that there are feasible alternatives to the present policy. What is lacking is not an alternative for Vietnam but the *desire* for one. Until such a desire becomes apparent—on the part of the present Administration or on the part of a new Administration—the rest of us can do little to influence the immediate course of events; we can, however, with longer term purposes in mind, be thinking about the essential factors involved in the war and their broader implications as to the kind of country America is and the kind of country we want it to be.

The essential question as to our war aims in Vietnam is quite simple: Do we want a total victory or a compromise? The Administration says, or used to say, that it wanted a compromise. At the same time it continues to expand the war and now refuses to negotiate on condition of suspending the bombing of North Vietnam—a condition that it said it would accept a year ago. In addition, our Administration and the Saigon government have made it clear that there can be no place for the National Liberation Front in a future South Vietnamese government; a high State Department official recently told me that that was a concession which the President could not be expected to make. It seems clear, therefore, that there is nothing to no gotiate, from our point of view, except the terms of our enemy's surrender.

When the Administration speaks of a *compromise*, it is really referring to an *amnesty*. Its South Vietnamese protégés indicated that they would allow individual members of a disbanded National Liberation Front to participate in the country's politics. What that means, assuming it can be taken at face value, is that they would not slaughter or permanently imprison the soldiers of the Vietcong and their political leaders but would allow them to live as citizens in a totally non-Communist South Vietnam. That is in the nature not of a compromise but of a surrender to be followed by an amnesty.

Underlying the current controversy about Vietnam are broader questions about the world-wide commitments of the United States and the most fundamental question of what kind of a country we want America to be. I have some opinions about that but my principal purpose today is to put that question to you. It is *your* generation that is going to make something good or something bad of America in the next few decades. The events which made America a world power with world responsibilities cannot be undone; but there are still choices to be made about how we are to meet those responsibilities, and yours is the generation that is going to have to make them. You are going to have to decide whether you are more interested in the national glory or the public welfare, in a great empire or a great society.

I do not know what your choices are going to be but of one thing I am sure: You cannot be neutral on the matter of America's future. You cannot avoid responsibility for the way your country is run by passing off the burden to politicians and political scientists who are supposed to be professionals. You cannot do it because there are no professionals in the matter of how people ought to live their lives, which is exactly what politics is about. I have been a politician for most of my life: I know politicians, I like them, and I respect their craft, but I can assure you that none of us—at any level of responsibility—is wise enough to decide how future generations should live their lives, to decide what kind of country America ought to be.

You, the young educated generation, can of course make your decisions by default. You can leave Vietnam, China, Russia, nuclear proliferation, and the population explosion to the politicians, political scientists, and computers. If you do that, and if things don't go the way you think they should, you will have no legitimate complaint; those who refuse responsibility deserve what they get.

The essential question for Americans today is whether we want our country to be the world's policeman, the arbiter of every conflict, and therefore an imperial power, or whether we want it to be what it has sometimes been in the past, an intelligent and humane

J. W. FULBRIGHT
17

society whose principal contribution to the outside world has been the power of its own example, a nation which cooperates with other countries and with international bodies like the United Nations to maintain peace. I am disturbed by what I believe to be a drift toward the role of global policeman, but there is reason for encouragement in the stirring of the conscience of our younger generation; excesses such as draft-card burning are unwise and unrewarding, but peaceful and orderly protest is in the best American tradition, a mark of our democracy's continuing vitality.

For many Americans it seems hard to believe that this power and affluence of ours was largely an accident of history and geography; it almost seems as though the Lord must have intended it, as though our riches were a reward for virtue and our power a sign of some special mission we are meant to carry out, of what used to be called "manifest destiny." Being so fortunate, we have gotten an idea that we live under a star, that America will always be rich, secure, and preeminent.

The Greeks, the Romans, the Spaniards, the French, the British, and the Germans all thought at one time that they lived under a star, that their preeminence was predestined and permanent. But all of these great empires either fell or declined. Contrary to our comforting illusions, all of the evidence of history is that America is not under a star, that the Lord is exactly as interested—or as uninterested—in Americans as he is in Russians, Chinese, Brazilians, and Nigerians. My own belief is that America is not predestined to anything; we may fall like Greece and Rome or we may decline like Spain. Or maybe—just maybe—if we are very wise and very farsighted, we may escape the pattern of past empires and survive to play a new and different kind of role in the world. That, however, depends on ourselves, on what we choose to make of our country with its enormous human and material riches.

Our history is ambiguous; it has prepared us either to follow the traditional course of empire or to make our society an example of intelligence, decency, and humanity.

On the one hand there is the tolerance and humanity of Lincoln, who found it strange, in the words of his second inaugural, "that any man should dare to ask for a just God's assistance in wringing their bread from the sweat of other men's faces," but then added: "let us judge not, that we be not judged." On the other hand, there is the old spirit of "manifest destiny" as expressed at the time of our war with Spain by a future Senator named Albert Beveridge, who proclaimed Americans to be "a conquering race." "We must obey our blood and occupy new markets and if necessary new lands," he said, because "in the Almighty's infinite plan . . . debased civilizations and decaying races" must disappear "before the higher civilization of the nobler and more virile types of man."

Beveridge's colorful language is out of style these days but the spirit of a universal mission is still with us. Here are a few examples:

On October 4, 1966, President Johnson told a group of war veterans that "in due time, notwithstanding discouragement, we will secure liberty for all human beings, regardless of race, color, or creed."

On August 25, 1966, Secretary of State Rusk told

a Senate committee that the United States might use its armed forces against a country judged to be an aggressor—judged, that is, by the President or perhaps by the Secretary of State—even in the absence of a defense treaty, an American military presence, or the approval of Congress.

Another recent sign of our country's drift toward the role of a global policeman was the request by the Defense Department for $301.1 million for the purpose of building special ships, called Fast Deployment Logistics Ships, which would be "pre-positioned" in the Far East, the Middle East, and other possible trouble spots to facilitate immediate American military intervention whenever or wherever we might wish. The Defense Department requested money for seven of these ships as a first installment on thirty, which altogether would cost over $1 billion. In support of this request, the Commandant of the Marine Corps stated that, with their great sea power, the Navy and the Marine Corps give the United States "an opportunity to exert its influence over most of the land areas of the earth."

Led by Senator Russell of Georgia, the Senate Armed Services Committee has very wisely rejected the request for these special ships. As Senator Russell said, the proposal suggests that "we are going to be drawn into war in new places." And on March 21, Senator Russell said in the Senate: ". . . we should not unilaterally assume the function of policing the world . . . if it is easy to go anywhere and do anything, we will always be going somewhere and doing something."

Underlying attitudes and proposals such as these is

the idea—the arrogant idea—that America is the rightful master of other peoples' destinies. In 1895 Secretary of State Olney said of the Americas: "Today the United States is practically sovereign on this continent, and its fiat is law upon the subjects to which it confines its interposition. In the spring of 1967, in a briefing to Senate aides on Vietnam, Secretary of State Rusk made the same assertion in bolder and simpler terms, stating approximately, that when the United States puts its hand to a thing, something's got to give. He was speaking of the Vietnamese war.

Of that war, one of our country's most respected journalists, Mr. Arthur Krock, wrote in his final column before his retirement: "The United States acting on a new geopolitical concept of domestic security and an evangelistic concept of world stewardship of national self-determination, has almost discarded the most fundamental teaching of the foremost American military analysts by assuming the burden of a ground war between Asians in Asia."

As we move deeper into a global role shaped by that "evangelistic concept of world stewardship," the generation which will be leading America in future decades—your generation—ought to be asking some fundamental questions about where that role is going to lead us and, more important, whether that is the role you want for America.

As to the first of these questions—where the role of global policeman will take us—history suggests that it is amost certain to be somewhere other than where we intend. One of our leading historians, Professor Henry Steele Commager, has made the point that "wars rarely come because they are carefully planned and deliberately launched—not ours anyway—but because circumstances get out of control. They come, most of them, notwithstanding earnest and even sincere efforts to avoid them. To assume that statesmen, or military men, sitting in distant capitals, can manipulate the great, seething and tumultuous processes of history as they might manipulate pieces on a chessboard is to ignore the lessons of the past." The record, says Professor Commager, shows that we Americans "do not plan our wars; we blunder into them."

Neither George Washington nor George III wanted war in 1775. Nor did the farmer who fired the first shot at Concord expect that it would be "heard 'round the world." As late as 1776 Washington, John Adams, and Thomas Jefferson were expressing their opposition to both independence and war. But war came, and so did independence.

Few people wanted or expected war in 1812. The British were busy with Napoleon, and the American "war hawks" were a distinct minority, but the useless war came nonetheless. The treaty which ended it said nothing about neutral rights on the high seas, which were the reason America went to war, but, as it turned out, England and America never had another war and the issue between them took care of itself.

Neither the North nor the South wanted the Civil War. The South hoped to be allowed to go in peace and the North hoped the South would return to the fold. As Lincoln put it in his second inaugural: "Both parties deprecated war, but one of them would *make* war rather than let the nation survive, and the other would *accept*

war rather than let it perish, and the war came. . . .
Neither party expected for the war the magnitude or
the duration which it has already attained. . . .
Each looked for an easier triumph and a result less
fundamental and astounding."

Theodore Roosevelt said that the war with Spain
was "a splendid little war," but, as Professor Commager
points out, the war it led to was not at all splendid and
it took everyone by surprise. Having liberated the
Philippines from Spain, President McKinley decided it
was America's duty to "civilize" and "Christianize" the
Filipinos. Before this noble work could be undertaken,
it was necessary to send 120,000 American soldiers to
fight a jungle war against Filipino nationalists who did
not want to be "civilized" and "Christianized." That
war lasted three years and cost almost as many lives as
the war with Spain.

The First World War may be the one example of a
war we entered deliberately but, far from making the
world "safe for democracy" as we intended for it to do,
that war set in motion the events which led to the
Second World War.

The United States entered the Second World War
not by its own choice but by the choice of Japan. As
to the consequences of the war, it would be hard to
cite a single characteristic of our present day world as
representing the fulfillment of the war aims embodied in
the Atlantic Charter and the Charter of the United
Nations.

As we consider our future course in Vietnam and
our developing role as policeman for the world, we might
do well to remember that neither wars nor their conse-

quences are easily controlled, that indeed our history shows an almost perfect record of accidental wars with unforeseen consequences.

Even if there were some prospect of success in the role of global policeman the question would remain whether that is the role that young Americans will want for their country.

It is said that we are so rich and so strong that we can be the world's policeman and build the Great Society both at the same time. That may possibly be true, theoretically, but things certainly are not working out that way. The 89th Congress, which enacted so much important domestic legislation in 1965, enacted very little in 1966, and the 90th Congress, which convened in January of 1967, has enacted virtually none. This is true in part because of the unusual productivity of Congress in 1964 and 1965, in part because of Republican gains in the 1966 elections, but also because the Congress as a whole has lost interest in the Great Society and become, politically and psychologically, a "war Congress."

Obviously, the rising costs of the Vietnamese war have built up pressure for economies elsewhere. Congress in 1967 appropriated a supplemental $12.3 billion for military costs, principally for the war in Vietnam, because the regular defense budget for that fiscal year, a staggering sum of $58 billion, has been inadequate to meet the country's military expenses. Since we do not feel able to economize on military expenditures and are unwilling to reduce spending on such a life-and-death matter as beating the Russians to the moon—at a cost of $20 to $30 billion—there seems no alternative but to cut back on domestic welfare programs. We are therefore requiring the poor and the schoolchildren of America to pay a large part of the cost of the Vietnamese war.

The inspiration and commitment have disappeared from the Great Society, not only because of pressures on our material resources but also for lack of mental and spiritual resources. Politicians, like other people, have only one brain apiece, and it stands to reason that if they spend all their time thinking about one thing they are not going to be thinking about something else. The President simply cannot think about implementing the Great Society at home while he is supervising bombing missions over North Vietnam; nor is the Congress much inclined to debate—much less finance—expanded domestic programs when it is involved in debating—and paying for—an expanding war; nor can the American people be expected to think very hard or do very much about improving their schools and communities when they are worried about casualty lists and the danger of a wider war.

Just as there is something unseemly about an individual carrying all the burdens of the Community Chest and the PTA while his own children run wild, there is also something unseemly about a nation conducting a foreign policy that involves it in the affairs of most of the nations in the world while its cities are wracked by violence, its streets choked with traffic, its rivers open sewers, and its air unfit to breathe. There is something fishy, something unhealthy, about this kind of behavior. I do not think that a man can be genuinely responsible in one area of his life and neglectful in another. I am more inclined to believe that the man who makes the best contribution to his community is the one who begins by meeting his responsibilities to himself and to his own family. By analogy, it seems to me unnatural and unhealthy for a nation to be engaged in global crusades for some ostensible principle or ideal while neglecting the needs of its own people; indeed, it seems far more likely that the nation that does most to benefit humanity in the long run is the nation that begins by meeting the needs of that portion of humanity which resides within its own frontiers.

The great Judge Oliver Wendell Holmes said that the first lesson a judge had to learn was that he was not God. It is a lesson that every man and every nation also have to learn. For, as the English historian Herbert Buttterfield said, "The hardest strokes of Heaven fall in history upon those who imagine that they can control things in a sovereign manner, as though they were Kings of the earth, playing Providence not only for themselves but for the far future, reaching out into the future with the wrong kind of farsightedness."

There is therefore no escaping the decision that has to be made. Do you want an American empire or do you want an America which is a model of dignity and decency, deeply involved in the world, as it must be, in cooperation with other nations and especially through the United Nations, but not so deeply involved entirely on its own as to become the proprietor of some nations and a bully to others, all at the expense of its own people?

Obviously I have loaded the question because I am not neutral on these matters. I would like America to treat Communist countries according to their behavior rather than their ideology; I would like America to be the friend of social justice in the world, ready to contribute money and technical skills under international auspices but not to impose its own political values; and I would like America to offer the world a model of democracy and public well-being, to be, in the words of John Quincy Adams, "the well-wisher to the freedom and independence of all" but "the champion and vindicator only of her own."

The more important question is what kind of a country do *you* want America to be? It is difficult to assess the historical period one lives in, but it seems likely that the generation of Americans now having higher education are coming to their maturity at a time when a most fundamental choice will have to be made. Our history is ambivalent: It has conditioned us to become either a seeker after empire and glory or a civilized example for the world. The choice will be yours and you had better be thinking about it.

J. W. FULBRIGHT

Conflict in Vietnam and at Home

Robert F. Kennedy

THE reason I'm here is that someone sent me a history of this city. And I found out that it was founded by people from Chicago who came to Kansas to found a town named Boston which they later changed to Manhattan. So I knew I'd be right at home.

I am proud to come here at the invitation of Alfred M. Landon. I met him at the White House when he visited there. I know how highly President Kennedy respected Governor Landon, and the continuing contribution he made—and still makes—to the public life of the country.

I am also glad to come to the home state of another Kansan who wrote, "If our colleges and universities do not breed men who riot, who rebel, who attack life with all the youthful vision and vigor, then there is something wrong with our colleges. The more riots that come on college campuses, the better world for tomorrow."

The man who wrote these words was that notorious seditionist, William Allen White—the late editor of the Emporia *Gazette* and one of the giants of American journalism. He is an honored man today; but when he lived and wrote, he was often reviled on your campus and across the nation as an extremist—or worse. For he spoke as he believed. He did not conceal his concern in comforting words; he did not delude his readers or himself with false hopes and illusions. It is in this spirit that I wish to speak.

For this is a year of choice—a year when we choose not simply who will lead us, but where we wish to be led; the country we want for ourselves—and the kind we want for our children. If in this year of choice we fashion new politics out of old illusions, we insure for ourselves nothing but crisis for the future—and we bequeath to our children the bitter harvest of those crises.

For with all we have done, with all our immense power and richness, our problems seem to grow not less, but greater. We are in a time of unprecedented turbulence, of danger and questioning. It is at its root a question of the national soul. The President calls it "restlessness"; while cabinet officers and commentators tell us that America is deep in a malaise of the spirit—discouraging initiative, paralyzing will and action, dividing Americans from one another by their age, their views, and the color of their skins.

There are many causes. Some are in the failed promise of America itself: in the children I have seen, starving in Mississippi; idling their lives away in the ghetto; committing suicide in the despair of Indian reservations; or watching their proud fathers sit without work in the ravaged lands of Eastern Kentucky. Another cause is in our inaction in the face of danger. We seem equally unable to control the violent disorder within our cities—or the pollution and destruction of the country, of the water and land that we use and our children must inherit. And a third great cause of discontent is the course we are following in Vietnam: in a war which has divided Americans as they have not been divided since your state was called "bloody Kansas."

All this — questioning and uncertainty at home, divisive war abroad—has led us to a deep crisis of confidence: in our leadership, in each other, and in our very self as a nation.

Today I would speak to you of the third of those great crises: of the war in Vietnam. I come here, to this serious forum in the heart of the nation, to discuss with you why I regard our policy there as bankrupt: not on the basis of emotion, but fact; not, I hope, in clichés—but with a clear and discriminating sense of where the national interest really lies.

I do not want—as I believe most Americans do not want—to sell out American interests, to simply withdraw, to raise the white flag of surrender. That would be unacceptable to us as a country and as a people. But I am concerned—as I believe most Americans are concerned—that the course we are following at the present time is deeply wrong. I am concerned—as I believe most Americans are concerned—that we are acting as if no other nations existed, against the judgment and desires of neutrals and our historic allies alike. I am concerned—as I believe most Americans are concerned—that our present course will not bring victory; will not bring peace; will not stop the bloodshed; and will not advance the interests of the United States or the cause of peace in the world.

I am concerned that, at the end of it all, there will only be more Americans killed; more of our treasure spilled out; and because of the bitterness and hatred on every side of this war, more hundreds of thousands of Vietnamese slaughtered; so that they may say, as Tacitus said of Rome: "They made a desert, and called it peace."

And I do not think that is what the American spirit is really all about.

Let me begin this discussion with a note both personal and public. I was involved in many of the early decisions on Vietnam, decisions which helped set us on our present path. It may be that the effort was doomed from the start; that it was never really possible to bring all the people of South Vietnam under the rule of the successive governments we supported — governments, one after another, riddled with corruption, inefficiency, and greed; governments which did not and could not successfully capture and energize the national feeling of their people. If that is the case, as it well may be, then I am willing to bear my share of the responsibility, before history and before my fellow-citizens. But past error is no excuse for its own perpetuation. Tragedy is a tool for the living to gain wisdom, not a guide by which to live. Now as ever, we do ourselves best justice when we measure ourselves against ancient tests, as in the Antigone of Sophocles: "All men make mistakes, but a good man yields when he knows his course is wrong, and repairs the evil. The only sin is pride."

The reversals of the last several months have led our military to ask for 206,000 more troops. This weekend, it was announced that some of them—a "moderate" increase, it was said—would soon be sent. But isn't this exactly what we have always done in the past? If we examine the history of this conflict, we find the dismal story repeated time after time. Every time—at every crisis—we have denied that anything was wrong; sent more troops; and issued more confident communiques. Every time, we have been assured that this one last step would bring victory. And every time, the predictions and promises have failed and been forgotten, and the demand has been made again for just one more step up the ladder.

But all the escalations, all the last steps, have brought us no closer to success than we were before. Rather, as the scale of the fighting has increased, South Vietnamese society has become less and less capable of organizing or defending itself, and we have more and more assumed the whole burden of the war. In just three years, we have gone from 16,000 advisers to over 500,000 troops; from no American bombing North or South, to an air campaign against both, greater than that waged in all the European theater in World War II; from less than 300 American dead in all the years prior to 1965, to more than 500 dead in a single week of combat in 1968.

And once again the President tells us, as we have been told for twenty years, that "we are going to win"; "victory" is coming.

ROBERT F. KENNEDY
33

But what are the true facts? What is our present situation?

First, our control over the rural population—so long described as the key to our efforts—has evaporated. The Vice-President tells us that the pacification program has "stopped." In the language of other high officials, it is a "considerable setback," with "loss of momentum," "some withdrawal from the countryside," "a significant psychological setback both on the part of pacification people themselves and the local population." Reports from the field indicate that the South Vietnamese Army has greatly increased its tendency to "pull into its compounds in cities and towns, especially at night, reduce its patrolling, and leave the militia and revolutionary development cadres open to enemy incursion and attack." Undoubtedly, this is one reason why, over two recent weeks, our combat deaths—1049—were so much greater than those of the South Vietnamese—557. Like it or not, the government of South Vietnam is pursuing an enclave policy. Its writ runs where American arms protect it: that far and no farther. To extend the power of the Saigon government over its own country, we now can see, will be in essence equivalent to the reconquest and occupation of most of the entire nation.

Let us clearly understand the full implications of that fact. The point of our pacification operations was always described as "winning the hearts and minds" of the people. We recognized that giving the countryside military security against the Viet Cong would be futile— indeed that it would be impossible—unless the people of the countryside themselves came to identify their interests with ours, and to assist not the Viet Cong, but the Saigon government. For this we recognized that their minds would have to be *changed*—that their natural inclination would be to support the Viet Cong, or at best remain passive, rather than sacrifice for foreign white men, or the remote Saigon government.

It is this effort that has been most gravely set back in the last month. We cannot change the minds of people in villages controlled by the enemy. The fact is, as all recognize, that we cannot reassert control over those villages now in enemy hands without repeating the whole process of bloody destruction which has ravaged the countryside of South Vietnam throughout the last three years. Nor could we thus keep control without the presence of millions of American troops. If, in the years those villages and hamlets were controlled by Saigon, the government had brought honesty, social reform, land reform—if that had happened, if the many promises of a new and better life for the people had been fulfilled—then in the process of reconquest, we might appear as liberators: just as we did in Europe, despite the devastation of war, in 1944-45. But the promises of reform were not kept. Corruption and abuse of administrative power have continued to this day. Land reform has never been more than an empty promise. Viewing the performances of the Saigon government over the last three years, there is no reason for the South Vietnamese peasant to fight for the extension of its authority or to view the further devastation that effort will bring as anything but a calamity. Yet already the destruction has defeated most of our own purposes. Arthur Gardiner is the former chief of the United States AID mission in South Vietnam, and currently executive director of the International Voluntary Services. He tells us that we are "creating more Viet Cong than we are destroying"—and "increasing numbers of Vietnamese are becoming benevolently neutral toward the Viet Cong." As a consequence, the political war—so long described as the only war that counts—has gone with the pacification program that was to win it. In a real sense, it may now be lost beyond recall.

The second evident fact of the last several months is that the Saigon government is no more or better an ally than it was before; that it may even be less; and that the war inexorably is growing more, not less, an American effort. American officials continue to talk about a government newly energized, moving with "great competence," taking hold "remarkably well," doing "a very, very good piece of work of recovery." I was in the executive branch of the government from 1961 to 1964. In all those years, we heard the same glowing promises about the South Vietnamese government: corruption would soon be eliminated, land reform would come, programs were being infused with new energy. But those were not the facts then, and they are not the facts today. The facts are that there is still no total mobilization: no price or wage controls, no rationing, no overtime work. The facts are, as a Committee of the House of Representatives has told us, that land reform is moving backward, with the government forces helping landlords to collect exorbitant back rents from the peasantry. The facts are that 18-year-old South Vietnamese are still not being drafted; though now, as many times in the past, we are assured that this will happen soon. The facts are that thousands of young South Vietnamese buy their deferments from military service while American marines die at Khe Sanh.

The facts are that the government has arrested monks and labor leaders, former Presidential candidates, and government officials—including prominent members of the Committee for the Preservation of the Nation, in which American officials placed such high hopes.

Meanwhile, the government's enormous corruption continues, debilitating South Vietnam and crippling our effort to help its people. Committees of the Senate and House of Representatives have officially documented the existence, extent, and results of this corruption: American AID money stolen, food diverted from refugees, government posts bought and sold while essential tasks remain undone. A subcommittee of the Senate Committee on Government Operations has reported that the Vietnamese collector of customs had engaged in smuggling gold and opium—and that he was protected by figures even higher in the government. President Johnson has responded to criticism of corruption in Vietnam by reminding us that there is stealing in Beaumont, Texas. I for one do not believe that Beaumont is so corrupt. I do not believe that any public official, in any American city, is engaged in smuggling gold and dope; selling draft deferments; or pocketing millions of dollars in U. S. government funds. But however corrupt any city in the United States may be, that corruption is not costing the lives of American soldiers; while the pervasive corruption of the government of Vietnam, as an American official has told us, is a significant cause of the prolongation of the war and the continued American casualties. As this government continues on its present course, and our support for it continues, the effect can only be to leave us totally isolated from the people of Vietnam. Our fighting men deserve better than that.

Third, it is becoming more evident with every passing day that the victories we achieve will only come at the cost of destruction for the nation we once hoped to help. Even before this winter, Vietnam and its people were disintegrating under the blows of war. Now hardly a city in Vietnam has been spared from the new ravages of the past few months. Saigon officials say that nearly three-quarters of a million new refugees have been created, to add to the existing refugee population of two million or more. No one really knows the number of civilian casualties. The city of Hue, with most of the country's cultural and artistic heritage, lies in ruins: Of its population of 145,000, fully 113,000 are said to be homeless. There is not enough food, not enough shelter, not enough medical care. There is only death and misery and destruction.

An American commander said of the town of Ben Tre, "It became necessary to destroy the town in order to save it." It is difficult to quarrel with the decision of American commanders to use air power and artillery to save the lives of their men; if American troops are to fight for Vietnamese cities, they deserve protection. What I cannot understand is why the responsibility for the recapture and attendant destruction of Hue, and Ben Tre and the others, should fall to American troops in the first place.

If Communist insurgents or invaders held New York or Washington or San Francisco, we would not leave it to foreigners to take them back, and destroy them and their people in the process. Rather I believe there is not one among us who would not tear the invaders out with his bare hands, whatever the cost. There is no question that some of the South Vietnamese army fought with great bravery. The Vietnamese—as these units, and the Viet Cong have both shown us—are a courageous people. But it is also true that a thousand South Vietnamese soldiers, in Hue on leave for Tet, hid among the refugees for three weeks, making no attempt to rejoin their units or join the town's defense; among them was a full colonel. And it is also true that in the height of the battle for Hue, as trucks brought back American dead and wounded from the front lines, millions of Americans could see, on their television screens, South Vietnamese soldiers occupied in looting the city those Americans were fighting to recapture.

If the government's troops will not or cannot carry the fight for their cities, we cannot ourselves destroy them. That kind of salvation is not an act we can presume to perform for them. For we must ask our government—we must ask ourselves: where does such logic end? If it becomes "necessary" to destroy all of South Vietnam in order to "save" it, will we do that too? And if we care so little about South Vietnam that we are willing to see the land destroyed and its people dead, then why are we there in the first place?

Can we ordain to ourselves the awful majesty of God—to decide what cities and villages are to be destroyed, who will live and who will die, and who will join the refugees wandering in a desert of our own creation? If it is true that we have a commitment to the South Vietnamese people, we must ask, are they being consulted—in Hue, or Ben Tre, or in the villages from which the three million refugees have fled? If they believe all the death and destruction are a lesser evil than the Viet Cong, why did they not warn us when the Viet Cong came into Hue, and the dozens of other cities, before the Tet offensive? Why did they not join the fight?

Will it be said of us, as Tacitus said of Rome: "They made a desert, and called it peace"?

It is also said that we are protecting Thailand—or perhaps Hawaii—from the legions of the Communists. Are we really protecting the rest of Southeast Asia by this spreading conflict? And in any case, is the destruction of South Vietnam and its people a permissible means of defense?

Let us have no misunderstanding. The Viet Cong are a brutal enemy indeed. Time and time again, they have shown their willingness to sacrifice innocent civilians, to engage in torture and murder and despicable terror to achieve their ends. This is a war almost without rules or quarter. There can be no easy moral answer to this war, no one-sided condemnation of American actions. What we must ask ourselves is whether we have a right to bring so much destruction to another land, without clear and convincing evidence that this is what its people want. But that is precisely the evidence we do not have. What they want is peace, not dominated by any outside force. And that is what we are really committed to help bring them, not in some indefinite future, but while some scraps of life remain still to be saved from the holocaust.

The fourth fact that is now more clear than ever is

that the war in Vietnam, far from being the last critical test for the United States, is in fact weakening our position in Asia and around the world, and eroding the structure of international cooperation which has directly supported our security for the past three decades. In purely military terms, the war has already stripped us of the graduated-response capability that we have labored so hard to build for the last seven years. Surely the North Koreans were emboldened to seize the Pueblo because they knew that the United States simply cannot afford to fight another Asian war while we are so tied down in Vietnam. We set out to prove our willingness to keep our commitments everywhere in the world. What we are ensuring instead is that it is most unlikely that the American people would ever again be willing to engage in this kind of struggle. Meanwhile our oldest and strongest allies pull back to their own shores, leaving us alone to police all of Asia; while Mao Tse-Tung and his Chinese comrades sit patiently by, fighting us to the last Vietnamese: watching us weaken a nation which might have provided a stout barrier against Chinese expansion southward; hoping that we will further tie ourselves down in protracted war in Cambodia, Laos, Thailand; confident, as it is reported from Hong Kong, that the war in Vietnam "will increasingly bog down the United States, sapping its resources, discrediting its power pretensions, alienating its allies, fraying its ties with the Soviet Union, and aggravating dissensions among Americans at home." As one American observer puts it, truly "We seem to be playing the script the way Mao wrote it."

All this bears directly and heavily on the question

of whether more troops should now be sent to Vietnam—and, if more are sent, what their mission will be. We are entitled to ask—we are required to ask—how many more men, how many more lives, how much more destruction will be asked, to provide the military victory that is always just around the corner, to pour into this bottomless pit of our dreams?

But this question the administration does not and cannot answer. It has no answer—none but the ever-expanding use of military force and the lives of our brave soldiers, in a conflict where military force has failed to solve anything in the past. The President has offered to negotiate—yet this weekend he told us again that he seeks not compromise but victory, "at the negotiating table if possible, on the battlefield if necessary." But at a real negotiating table, there can be no "victory" for either side; only a painful and difficult compromise. To seek victory at the conference table is to ensure that you will never reach it. Instead the war will go on, year after terrible year—until those who sit in the seats of high policy are men who seek another path. And that must be done this year.

For it is long past time to ask: what is this war doing to us? Of course it is costing us money—fully one-fourth of our federal budget—but that is the smallest price we pay. The cost is in our young men, the tens of thousands of their lives cut off forever. The cost is in our world position—in neutrals and allies alike, every day more baffled by and estranged from a policy they cannot understand.

Higher yet is the price we pay in our own innermost lives, and in the spirit of our country. For the first time in a century, we have open resistance to service in the cause of the nation. For the first time perhaps in our history, we have desertions from our army on political and moral grounds. The front pages of our newspapers show photographs of American soldiers torturing prisoners. Every night we watch horror on the evening news. Violence spreads inexorably across the nation, filling our streets and crippling our lives. And whatever the costs to us, let us think of the young men we have sent there: not just the killed, but those who have to kill; not just the maimed, but also those who must look upon the results of what they do.

It may be asked, is not such degradation the cost of all wars? Of course it is. That is why war is not an enterprise lightly to be undertaken, nor prolonged one moment past its absolute necessity. All this—the destruction of Vietnam, the cost to ourselves, the danger to the world—all this we would stand willingly, if it seemed to serve some worthwhile end. But the costs of the war's present course far outweigh anything we can reasonably hope to gain by it, for ourselves or for the people of Vietnam. It must be ended, and it can be ended, in a peace of brave men who have fought each other with a terrible fury, each believing he and he alone was in the right. We have prayed to different gods, and the prayers of neither have been answered fully. Now, while there is still time for some of them to be partly answered, now is the time to stop.

And the fact is that much can be done. We can— as I have urged for two years, but as we have never done —negotiate with the National Liberation Front. We can—as we have never done—assure the Front a genuine place in the political life of South Vietnam. We can — as we are refusing to do today — begin to de-escalate the war, concentrate on protecting populated areas, and thus save American lives and slow down the destruction of the countryside. We can—as we have never done—insist that the government of South Vietnam broaden its base, institute real reforms, and seek an honorable settlement with their fellow countrymen.

This is no radical program of surrender. This is no sell-out of American interests. This is a modest and reasonable program, designed to advance the interests of this country and save something from the wreckage for the people of Vietnam.

This program would be far more effective than the present course of this Administration—whose only response to failure is to repeat it on a larger scale. This program, with its more limited costs, would indeed be far more likely to accomplish our true objectives.

And therefore even this modest and reasonable program is impossible while our present leadership, under the illusion that military victory is just ahead, plunges deeper into the swamp that is our present course.

So I come here to ask your help: not for me, but for your country and for the people of Vietnam. You are the people, as President Kennedy said, who have "the least ties to the present and the greatest ties to the future." I urge you to learn the harsh facts that lurk behind the mask of official illusion with which we have concealed our true circumstances, even from ourselves. Our country is in danger: not just from foreign enemies; but above all, from our own misguided policies—and what they can do to the nation that Thomas Jefferson once told us was the last, best, hope of man. There is a contest on, not for the rule of America, but for the heart of America. In these next eight months, we are going to decide what this country will stand for—and what kind of men we are. So I ask for your help, in the cities and homes of this state, in the towns and farms: contributing your concern and action, warning of the danger of what we are doing—and the promise of what we can do. I ask you, as tens of thousands of young men and women are doing all over this land, to organize yourselves, and then to go forth and work for new policies—work to change our direction—and thus restore our place at the point of moral leadership, in our country, in our hearts, and all around the world.

The Future
of Integration

Martin Luther King, Jr.

THERE seems to be a desperate, poignant question on the lips of thousands and millions of people all over our nation and all over the world. They are asking whether we have made any real progress in the area of race relations.

In seeking to answer this question I always seek to avoid, on the one hand, a superficial optimism and, on the other hand, a deadening pessimism. I always try to answer it by giving what I consider a realistic position. It seems to me that the realistic position is that we have made significant strides in the struggle for racial justice, but that we have a long, long way to go before the problem is solved. And so, as I think about the civil rights movement, and as I think about the future of integration, I would like to use this realistic position as the basis for our thinking together.

We have come a long, long way but we still have a long, long way to go before we have a truly integrated and just society. Now there is no disagreement that we have come a long, long way. And I would like to point out that the Negro, himself, has come a long, long way in re-evaluating his own intrinsic worth. In order to illustrate this a little history is necessary.

You will remember that it was in the year 1619 when the first Negro slaves landed on the shores of this nation. They were brought here from the soils of Africa. And unlike the Pilgrim fathers who landed at Plymouth a year later, they were brought here against their will.

Throughout slavery the Negro was treated in a very inhuman fashion. He was a thing to be used, and not a person to be respected. The famous Dred Scott decision of 1857 well illustrated the status of the Negro during slavery. With this decision the Supreme Court of the United States said in substance that the Negro is not a citizen of the United States—that he is merely property, subject to the dictates of his owner. And it went on to say that the Negro had no rights that the white man is bound to respect.

With the growth of slavery it became necessary to give some justification for it. It seems to be a fact of life that human beings cannot continue to do wrong without eventually reaching out for some thin rationalization to clothe an obvious wrong in the beautiful garments of righteousness. This is exactly what happened. Indeed, religion and the Bible were used—or I should say misused—in order to justify the system of slavery. And so it was argued that the Negro was inferior by nature because of Noah's curse upon the children of Ham. The apostle Paul's dictum became a watchword: "Servants, be obedient to them that are your masters."

One brother had probably read the logic of the great philosopher Aristotle. Aristotle did a good deal to bring into being what we now know as formal logic in philosophy. And in formal logic there is a big word called a "syllogism" which has a major premise, a minor premise, and a conclusion. And so this brother put his arguments of the inferiority of the Negro in the framework of an Aristotelian syllogism. He came out with his major premise that all men are made in the image of God. Then came his minor premise: God as everybody knows is not Negro; therefore the Negro is not a man. This is the kind of reasoning that prevailed.

While living with the conditions of slavery, and then later with humiliating patterns of segregation, many Negroes lost faith in themselves. Many came to feel that perhaps they were inferior; perhaps they were less than human.

But then something happened to the Negro. Circumstances made it possible and necessary for him to travel more — the coming of the automobile, the upheavals of two world wars, the great depression. So his rural plantation background gradually gave way to urban industrial life. His cultural life was gradually rising, too, with the steady decline of crippling illiteracy. He watched with a deep sense of pride the great drama of his independence taking place on the stage of African history. And all of these forces conjoined to cause the Negro to take a new look at himself.

Negro Americans all over began to re-evaluate themselves, and the Negro came to feel that he was somebody. His religion revealed to him that God loves all of His children, and that all men are made in His image, and that the basic thing about a man is not the specifics but the fundamentals—not the texture of his hair, nor the color of his skin, but his eternal dignity and worth.

So the Negro, with his fleecy locks and black complexion, could now unconsciously cry out with eloquent force that man cannot forfeit nature's claims. Skin may differ, but affection dwells in black and white the same. If I were so tall as to reach the Pole or to grasp the ocean at a span, I must be measured by my soul.

The mind is the standard of a man, and with this new sense of dignity, and this new sense of self-respect, a new Negro came into being with new determination to struggle, to suffer, and to sacrifice in order to be free. And so we have come a long, long way since 1619.

But if we are to be true to the fact, it is necessary to point out that the whole nation has made strides in extending the frontiers of democracy, the frontiers of civil rights. And there are many things I could say at this point, but time will only permit me to mention one basic change that we have seen over the last ten or twelve years.

We have seen an absolute crumbling of the system of legal segregation which pervaded so much of the South and the border states for so many, many years. We all know the history of the system of segregation. It had its legal beginning in 1896 when the Supreme

Court rendered a decision as the *Plessey* vs. *Ferguson* decision. This established the doctrine of "separate but equal" as the law of the land.

Of course, we all know what happened as a result of the Plessey doctrine. There was always a strict enforcement of the "separate," without the slightest intention to abide by the "equal." The Negro ended up being plunged into the abyss of exploitation where he experienced the bleakness of nagging injustice.

But something else happened; it was on May 17, 1954. On that date, after examining the legal body of segregation, the United States Supreme Court pronounced it constitutionally dead. It said in substance that the old Plessey doctrine must go: that separate facilities are inherently unequal—that to segregate a child on the basis of his race is to deny that child equal protection of the law.

After that legal turning point, we noticed the psychological turning point where people by the thousands began to act. They started engaging in direct actions to fulfill the real ends expressed in the legal turning point. So there was the bus boycott in Montgomery, Alabama, in 1956, where 50,000 Negroes decided that it was ultimately more honorable to walk the streets in dignity than to accept segregation and humiliation in the midst of the conditions of life. Then, in 1960, the student movement came into being—the "sit-in" movement. By the thousands, students and adults sat in at lunch counters in order to protest segregated conditions. When they sat in at those lunch counters, they were in reality standing up for the best in the American dream and carrying the whole nation back to those wells of democracy which were dug deep by the founding fathers in the formulation of the Constitution and the Declaration of Independence. Then came other movements like the Birmingham movement, the Selma movement.

All of these movements, over the last ten years, had a powerful impact in bringing an end to legal segregation and the humiliation surrounding that system. So we have seen many changes as a result of the Civil Rights Act of 1964 and the Voting Rights Act of 1965. We have come a long, long way since 1896.

Now this would be a very good place for me to end my speech. First, it would mean making a relatively short speech, and that would be a magnificent accomplishment for a Baptist preacher. But beyond that, it would mean that the problem is just about solved now, and that we really don't have much to do. It would be a wonderful thing if speakers all over our country could talk about the problem of racial injustice in terms of a problem that once existed but no longer exists. But if I stop at this point, I would merely be stating a fact and not telling the truth.

You see, a fact is merely the absence of contradiction, but truth is the presence of coherence. Truth is the relatedness of facts. Now it is a fact that we have come a long, long way, but it isn't the whole truth. And if I stopped at this point, I am afraid I would leave you the victims of an illusion wrapped in superficiality, and we would all go away the victims of a dangerous optimism. And so, in order to tell the truth, it is necessary to move on, and not only to talk about the problem in terms of the progress that we have made, but also to make it clear that we still have a long, long way to go before the problem of racial injustice is solved.

We don't have to look very far to see this. We merely need to look around in our communities, to open our newspapers, and to turn on our televisions. Day in and day out, we are reminded of the fact that no area of our country can boast of clean hands in the realm of brotherhood.

Sometimes, the tragedies of racial injustice are expressed with more overt expressions of man's inhumanity to man as ugly violence. There are some counties in the deep South where murder of a civil rights worker, whether he be white or black, is still a popular pastime. In the state of Mississippi, for instance, over the last four years, more than sixty-two Negro or white civil rights workers have been brutally murdered, and not a single person has been convicted for these dastardly crimes. A few days ago, some were convicted in reference to the murder of three civil rights workers in 1964. We must remember that they were not convicted for murder on the state level. They were convicted through a Federal conspiracy law. No one has yet been convicted in the state of Mississippi for these sixty-two murders that I mentioned earlier.

Over the last two years, some fifty Negro churches have been burned to the ground in the state of Mississippi. Nothing has been done about it. It seems that they have a new motto in Mississippi now—not "Attend the church of your choice," but "Burn the church of your choice." Oh, how tragic this is! It tells us that we still have a long, long way to go.

MARTIN LUTHER KING, JR.

The problem does not end with physical violence. There is another kind of violence; there is another kind of murder that is as injurious as physical violence to the person that it is inflicted upon. It is possible to lynch an individual psychologically and spiritually. And by the millions in the ghettos of our nation, North and South, Negroes are being murdered and lynched every day in the spiritual and psychological sense.

We must not overlook the fact that more than 34 per cent of the Negro families of our country live in substandard housing conditions. In most instances, they do not have wall-to-wall carpets, but rather wall-to-wall rats and roaches. Conditions are so depressing that they would humiliate anyone facing them.

And all over our country, young Negro students are forced to attend inadequate, overcrowded, segregated schools. That is not only still true of the South, but it is still true all over the country. So often, year after year, thousands of Negro boys and girls finish high school reading at an eighth or ninth grade level— not because they are dumb, not because they do not have native intelligence, but because the schools are so inadequate, so overcrowded, so devoid of quality, so segregated if you will, that the best in these minds have never come out.

Then there is the other problem, which is probably the most crucial problem—namely, the economic problem. The vast majority of Negroes in America are still perishing on a lonely island of poverty in the midst of a vast ocean of material prosperity. More than 40 per cent of the Negro families of our country are poverty stricken, in the sense that they make wages less than the poverty level. Eighty-nine per cent of the Negro families of America earn less than $7,000 a year.

The unemployment rate in the Negro community is still at a depression level. Government figures would say that unemployment in Negro communities is about 8.8 per cent nationally, but these figures would only deal with individuals who were once in the labor market and who still go down to the employment office to try to find a job. These figures do not deal with what we refer to as the discouraged—thousands and thousands who have given up, who have lost hope, who have had so many defeats and so many doors closed in their faces that they have lost motivation—the people who have come to feel that life is a long and desolate corridor with no exit signs. If you add these, the unemployment rate would probably be 16 or 17 per cent of the Negro community. And when we come to Negro youth the unemployment rate is between 30 and 50 per cent. In some cities it goes as high as 50 per cent.

I was working in Cleveland last summer with our organization, and day after day I would walk through the hub area which is the Negro ghetto. It didn't take me long to discover that 15 per cent of the people, the adults in the hub, are unemployed. It didn't take me long to discover that 58 per cent of the young Negro men of Cleveland are either unemployed or make wages below the poverty level. This can be duplicated in cities all over America.

The problem is not only unemployment but it is underemployment. The fact is that most of the poverty stricken people in our country work every day, but they make wages so low that they cannot begin to function in the mainstream of economic life of our nation. They work in our hospitals; they work in our hotels; they work in our laundries. The vast majority of them are in domestic service—working every day, long hours, and yet earning so little that they cannot begin to function in the mainstream of the economic life of the nation. This has made for a great deal of despair.

The economic, the housing, the educational problems have made for a great deal of bitterness. We have seen angry explosions of this bitterness in the form of violence over the last two or three summers.

I need not give a long explanation or exposition of my position on the question of violence versus non-violence. I am still convinced that non-violence is the most potent weapon available to oppressed people in their struggle for freedom and human dignity. I am still convinced that violence creates many more social problems than it solves. And if the Negro in America succumbs to the temptation of using violence as his problematic strategy, unborn generations will be the recipients of a long and desolate night of bitterness. And our chief legacy to the future will be an endless strain of meaningless chaos.

So I will continue to raise my voice against violence, against riots, because they tend to intensify the fears of the white majority, while relieving their guilt. And we need a method that will somehow disarm the opponent, expose his moral defenses, and at the same time work on his conscience.

But after saying this, I must say that it would be an act of moral irresponsibility for me to condemn riots and not be as vigorous in condemning the continued existence of intolerable conditions in our society, which cause people to feel so angry and bitter that they conclude they have no alternative to get attention but to engage in this kind of violence.

What we must see is that a riot is the language of the unheard. And what is it that America has failed to hear? She has failed to hear that the plight of the Negro poor has worsened over the last few years. She has failed to hear the promises of freedom and equality that have not been met. America has failed to hear that large segments of white society are more concerned about tranquility and the status quo than about justice, humanity, and equality. And so it is still true that our nation's summers of riots are caused by our nation's winters of delay. As long as justice is postponed, we will be on the verge of social destruction.

Now let me rush on to say that if we are to go the additional distance to make justice a reality, and truly integrated society a reality, we are going to have to do something about it. And may I remind you that the struggle now is much more difficult. Over the last ten or twelve years, we were struggling to end segregation and the syndrome of deprivation surrounding that system. Many people supported us in that struggle. They were honestly outraged when they saw the brutality that we faced from a Jim Clark in Selma, or a Bull Connor in Birmingham. So out of a sense of decency they rose up and supported that struggle.

Some of the people that have supported that struggle are not supporting it so well today. It really boils down to the fact that they were doing the right thing for the wrong reason. T. S. Eliot says somewhere that there is no greater heresy than to do the right thing for the wrong reason. A lot of people supported us in Selma and Birmingham because they were against Bull Connor and they were against Jim Clark—and not because they were for genuine equality for the black man. And the new era of the struggle is now a struggle for genuine equality.

A lot of people supported us there in those struggles because it didn't cost the nation anything. It did not cost the nation one penny to integrate lunch counters. In fact, it helped the business community. It did not cost the nation one penny to guarantee the right to vote or to have access to public accommodation. And now we are dealing with problems that can only be solved by the nation providing billions of dollars to do it. Therefore, it is much easier to integrate a lunch counter than it is to eradicate slums. It is easier to guarantee the right to vote than it is to guarantee an annual income. And yet these are the better things that must be tackled.

If the problem is to be solved in the days ahead, let me make some suggestions about things that I consider necessary. If we are going this additional distance, we are in dire need of a massive action program all over our country to get rid of the last vestiges of racism and its external effects. In short, the problem will not work itself out. We must continue to work at it with zeal and with determination.

In order to develop the kind of action programs that I am thinking about, we must get rid of two or three myths that are still being disseminated around our society. One is what I refer to as the "myth of time."

I am sure you have heard this notion. It is the notion that only time can solve the problem. And I know there are those sincere people who say to civil rights leaders and persons working for civil rights, "You are pushing things too fast; you must slow up for a while.'" And then they have a way of saying: "Now just be nice and be patient and continue to pray, and in a hundred or two hundred years the problem will work itself out, because only time can solve the problem."

Well, I think there is an answer to that myth. And it is that time is neutral. Time can either be used constructively or destructively. And I am sad to say that I am absolutely convinced that the forces of ill will in our nation, the people on the wrong side in our nation— the extreme rightists of our nation, have often used time much more effectively than the people of good will. And it may well be that we may have to repent in this generation, not merely for the vitriolic words and violent action of the bad people, but for the appalling silence and indifference of the good people who sit around and say "wait on time."

Somewhere, we must come to see that human progress never rolls in on the wheels of inevitability. It comes through the tireless effort and the persistent work of dedicated individuals who are willing to be co-workers with God. Without this hard work, time itself becomes an ally of the primitive forces of social stagnation.

And there is another myth that is disseminated a great deal. It is the notion that legislation has no role to play in establishing justice and in moving toward an integrated society. The argument here is that you must change the heart of man and you cannot change the heart through legislation. You cannot legislate morals. I would be the first one to say that hearts must be changed.

I said earlier that I am a Baptist preacher. That means that I am in the heart-changing business. I preach Sunday after Sunday about the need for conversion and regeneration—the new birth, so to speak. So I believe in the changing of hearts. I realize that, if we are to have a truly integrated society, white people are going to have to treat Negro people right—not just because the law says it, but because it is natural, and because it is right, and because the Negro is the white man's brother. I would be the first to say that we will never have a truly integrated and brotherly society until men and women rise to the majestic heights of being obedient to the unenforceable.

But after saying that, I must point out the other side. It may be true that morality can not be legislated. But behavior can be regulated. It may be true that the law cannot change the heart. But it can restrain the heartless. It may be true that the law can not make a man love me. But it can restrain him from lynching me, and I think that is pretty important, also. And so while the law may not change the hearts of men, the law can change the habits of men if it is vigorously enforced.

There is need for civil rights legislation all over the country in various areas—in the economic area, still in the educational area, and in the housing area.

There is a great problem facing our nation today, and we see it in almost every city in the country. It is the constant growth of predominantly Negro central cities, ringed by white suburbs. If the pattern continues, it will invite social disaster. The only way this problem can be solved is through strong fair housing bills. Right here in the state of Kansas this issue is being dealt with, but there are still recalcitrant forces seeking to defeat a fair housing bill which this state desperately needs. And I am so happy that there are those who are working with determination to bring this into being. Every state in this Union needs a fair housing bill that will make it possible for people to live together and not face discrimination in housing.

Another myth surrounding us is what I call an exaggerated use of the "boot-strap" philosophy. People say to the Negroes: "You must lift yourself by your own boot straps." So often I hear people saying: "The Irish, Italians—and they go right down the line of all other ethnic groups—came to this country and faced problems. They had difficulties, and yet they lifted themselves by their own boot straps. Why can't and why won't the Negro do this?"

It does not help the Negro for unfeeling, insensitive whites to say to him that ethnic groups that voluntarily came to this country 150 years ago have now risen beyond the Negro, who has been here more than 344 years but was brought here in chains involuntarily. The people who project this argument never seem to realize that no other ethnic groups have been slaves on American soil. They do not stop to realize that America made the Negro's color a stigma.

Making color a stigma had the support of the semantics or linguistics structure, so to speak. Even the language conspired to give the Negro the impression that something was wrong with his color. Open *Roget's*

Thesaurus and you will see the 120 synonyms for "black." All of them are low and degrading, or represent smut or dirt. Then look at the 130 synonyms for "white." They are all high, noble, chaste, pure. So in our society when somebody goes wrong in the family, you don't call him a "white sheep"; you call him a "black sheep." If you tell a lie, it's better to tell a "white lie" than a "black lie," because a white lie is a little better. If you know something about somebody and you use that as a means of bribing him for money, and you would expose him if you don't get it, you don't call it "whitemail"—you call it "blackmail." Now this is a bit humorous, but it is a fact of life.

Many things conspired to make the Negro feel that he was nobody because of his color. But the other thing that refutes this myth is the notion that anybody, any ethnic group, lifted itself totally by its own boot straps.

The Negro was freed from the bondage of physical slavery in 1863 through the Emancipation Proclamation. But the Negro was not given any land to make that freedom meaningful. It was something like keeping someone in prison for many years, and then suddenly discovering that he is not guilty for the crime for which he was convicted. Then you go to him and say, "Now you are free," but you do not give him any bus fare to get to town, or any money to buy clothes to put on his back, or any money for shoes to put on his feet. Every code of jurisprudence is against this. And yet this is exactly what America did to the black man. In 1863 America just said, "You are free"; and he was left penniless, illiterate, with nothing.

Here is the story that is not often told. At the same

time America refused to give the Negro any land, by Act of Congress she was giving away millions of acres of land in the West and the Midwest, which meant that America was willing to undergird her white peasants from Europe with an economic floor. Not only did the nation give the land, it built land-grant colleges to teach these people how to farm. It provided county agents to further their expertise in farming. It provided low interest rates so that they could mechanize their farms. And today many of these people are being paid through federal subsidies *not* to farm.

These are the very people who, in many instances, are saying to the Negro that he should lift himself by his own boot straps. I guess this is all right to say to a man that he should lift himself by his own boot straps, but it is a cruel jest to say to a bootless man that he should lift himself by his own boot straps.

The nation has a debt that it must pay. The longer it refuses to pay that debt, the more problems there will be—the more we will see the crises in our cities, developing and developing. There should be a massive program, a kind of Bill of Rights for the disadvantaged, that will really grapple with the slums, the economic problem generally, and all the things that I have tried to outline. We have the resources as a nation to do that. The question is whether America has the will. I am afraid that we have such mixed-up priorities nationally that without hard work we will not respond to this crisis.

I submit to you today that we spend $500,000 for every Viet Cong we end up killing in Vietnam, and yet we spend only $53 a year for every person characterized as poverty stricken in the so-called war against poverty.

MARTIN LUTHER KING, JR.

I am afraid that the national administration is more concerned about winning what I consider an unjust, ill-considered war in Vietnam than it is about winning the war against poverty right here at home. I raise my voice against that war because I have seen the damage that it has done to our nation. I see values being corroded and destroyed every day as a result of the war in Vietnam. It has diverted attention from civil rights. It has strengthened the military-industrial complex. It has destroyed the Geneva Accords. It is a war that places our nation in a position of really being against the self-determination of the Vietnamese people. It has placed us in a position of being what Mr. Fulbright has called "arrogant," of being victimized with the arrogance of power. This war has played havoc with our domestic destiny. For all of these reasons I have to take a stand against it.

Somebody said to me not too long ago: "Dr. King, don't you feel that you will have to talk more in line with the administration's policy from now on, because many people who once respected you will lose respect for you and this will hurt the budget of your organization. Don't you think you are going to have to change and stop talking against the war?" And I had to look at that person and say: "I am sorry, sir, but you do not know me. I am not a consensus leader. I do not determine what is right and wrong by looking at the budget of my organization, or by taking a Gallup poll of majority opinion. Ultimately, a genuine leader is not a searcher for consensus but a molder of consensus."

On some positions, cowards ask the question: "Is it safe?" Expediency asks the question: "Is it politic?"

Vanity asks the question: "Is it popular?" But conscience asks the question: "Is it right?" There comes a time when one must take a position that is neither safe, nor politic, nor popular. He must take it because conscience tells him that he is right. And that is where I stand today. Suffice it to say the economic problem is real. If we are to go this additional distance, we must work passionately and unrelentingly.

There are certain technical words in every academic discipline that soon become stereotypes and clichés. Every academic discipline has its technical nomenclature. Modern psychology has a word that is probably used more than any other word in psychology. It is the word "maladjusted." This is the ringing cry of the child psychologist. Certainly we all want to avoid a maladjusted life in order to avoid neurotic or schizophrenic personalities. But there are some things in our society and in our world to which I am proud to be maladjusted —to which I call upon all men of good will to be maladjusted until the good society is realized.

I never intend to become adjusted to segregation and discrimination. I never intend to adjust myself to religious bigotry. I never intend to adjust myself to economic conditions that will take necessity from the many to give luxury to the few. I never intend to adjust myself to the madness of militarism or to the self-defeating effects of physical violence in a day when Sputniks, Explorers, and Geminis are dashing through outer space and guided ballistic missiles are carving highways of death through the stratosphere.

No nation can ultimately win a war. It is no longer a choice between violence and non-violence. It is either

MARTIN LUTHER KING, JR.

non-violence or non-existence. The alternative to disarmament, the alternative to a suspension of nuclear testing, the alternative to strengthening the United Nations and thereby disarming the whole world, may well be a civilization plunged into the abyss of annihilation. And our earthly habitat will be transformed into an inferno that even the mind of Dante could not envision.

Maybe our world is in dire need of a new organization, the International Association for the Advancement of Creative Maladjustment—an association of men and women who will be as maladjusted as the Prophet Amos who, in the midst of the injustices of his day, cried in words that echo across the centuries: "Let justice run down as waters, and righteousness as a mighty stream"; as maladjusted as Abraham Lincoln who, in the midst of his vacillations, finally came to see that this nation could not survive half-slave and half-free; as maladjusted as Thomas Jefferson who, in the midst of an age amazingly adjusted to slavery, etched across the pages of history words lifted to cosmic proportions: "We hold these truths to be self-evident, that all Men are created equal, that they are endowed by their Creator with certain unalienable Rights, that among these are Life, Liberty, and the Pursuit of Happiness"; as maladjusted as Jesus of Nazareth, who could say in the midst of the military machine of the Roman Empire: "All they that take the sword shall perish with the sword."

Through such maladjustment, we will be able to emerge from the bleak and desolate midnight of man's inhumanity to man, to the bright and glittering daybreak of freedom and justice.

I must admit that there are times when I get rather

discouraged in the midst of set-backs—in the midst of what I see as constant vacillations and ambivalences of American white society. There are times that some of us begin to wonder whether this problem can be solved. But whenever I go out and around the colleges and universities of our country, and talk with many young people, I must honestly say to you that my hope is always renewed in those settings. I think that you who sit today under the sound of my voice may well have the answer, for it is the student generation that is saying to America that there must be a radical reordering of priorities. It is the student generation that is saying to America there must be a revolution of values, and is forcing America to review its values.

President Johnson in his State of the Union message wondered why there is so much restlessness. He talked about material prosperity. He talked about the highways and the beautiful cars flowing on those highways. He talked about the seventy million television sets. And then he wanted to know why there is so much restlessness. I would like to answer the President by saying that there is restlessness in this society because we have allowed the means by which we live to outdistance the ends for which we live.

Young people are restless because they are tired of killing. They want to make love not war. Young people are restless today because they are tired of the processes that are unfolding. Our national purpose and our national priorities are being questioned, and I see the hope within the young people of our generation.

I conclude by saying our goal is freedom. And I believe we are going to get there. However much

America strays away from it, the goal of America is freedom.

Our destiny somehow is tied up with the destiny of America. Before the Pilgrim fathers landed at Plymouth, we were here. Before Jefferson wrote the beautiful words of the Declaration of Independence, we were here. Before the words of the Star Spangled Banner were written, we were here. And for more than two centuries our forebears labored here without wages. They made cotton kings, and they built the homes of their masters, in the midst of the most humiliating and oppressive conditions. Yet, out of bottomless vitality they continue to grow and develop. If the inexpressible coat of slavery could not stop us, the opposition that we now face—including the white backlash—will surely fail.

We are going to win our freedom, because both the sacred heritage of our nation and the eternal will of the Almighty God are embodied in our echoing demands.

And so I can still sing, "we shall overcome." We shall overcome because the universe bends toward justice. We shall overcome because Carlyle is right—no lie can live forever. We shall overcome because William Cullen Bryant is right—"Truth, crushed to earth, shall rise again." We shall overcome, because James Russell Lowell is right—"Truth forever on the scaffold, Wrong forever on the throne." Yet that scaffold sways the future.

With this faith we will be able to hew out of the mounting despair the stone of hope. With this faith we will be able to transform the jangling discords of our nation into a beautiful symphony of brotherhood. With this faith we will be able to speed up the day when all of God's children all over this nation—black men and white men, Jews and Gentiles, Protestants and Catholics—will be able to join hands and sing in the words of the old Negro spiritual, "Free at last! Free at last! Thank God Almighty! We are free at last!"

MARTIN LUTHER KING, JR.

New Challenges
in International Relations

Alfred M. Landon

WE must face the challenges of new realities of international life today.

The world is an armed camp. An uneasy peace is maintained, while a power struggle continues to build up between the Soviet Union and China, with the United States neutral between them. On the other hand, we support South Vietnam's opposition to Communist aggression.

India, the second largest nation, wrecked by socialistic leadership, is racked by internal dissension and menaced by external threats.

The potential colossus of China—the world's most populous nation — is experiencing a severe internal revolution.

The end of the Vietnam war is not in sight. And

the vital questions of barring the use and spread of nuclear weapons and the military use of space remain unanswered.

Everywhere, a new nationalism—having recently vanquished European empires — is now transcending ideologies and old alliances, and is paradoxically supporting world peace, based on fear—not trust. World Communism, the United Nations, NATO, and the Atlantic Alliance are fragmenting on the rocks of this new nationalism.

This new nationalism is one of independence and self-determination. It is not the old dynasty nationalism with its ancestral roots in medieval feudalism. Nor is it the aggressive nationalism of modern dictators built on the doctrine of force.

World War One wiped out the last of the monarchs representing the centuries-old dynasty nationalism. And World War Two eliminated two megalomaniac dictators—Hitler and Mussolini—and their Japanese brethren. The policies of two more aggressors—Stalin and Sukarno—have been thrown by their people on the scrap heap of history. Only one of the five megalomaniacs of our time is left—China's troubled Mao. The ruthless Red Guards turned loose by him on his unhappy countrymen are a sad re-creation of Hitler's Jackboots and Mussolini's Blackshirts.

Meanwhile, China's world influence has suffered severe reversals—in Latin America, Africa, India, and Indonesia—and also in the United Nations which, by the greatest majority vote in some years, recently refused to seat Communist China.

This new nationalism is transcending Communism.

Both outside—as well as inside China—the theories of Marx and Lenin for the establishment and maintenance of worldwide Communism are being revised. The turmoil in China is essentially concerned with a struggle between the fundamentalists and revisionists.

The Soviet Union is departing so far from the original concepts of Marx and Lenin as to render them almost unrecognizable. Soviet Communism is moving slowly and subtly, but surely, toward incorporation of certain capitalistic principles of reward for individual talent and incentive.

Behind the thinning and now porous Iron Curtain, Communism has failed to meet the hopes and aspirations of its people. Its hierarchy is changed. Developing public opinion has eroded and loosened its monolithic structure.

The heretofore captive East European satellites are no longer captive nor satellites. They are pushing away from economic and political control and domination by Moscow. And it must be admitted that—by the same token—Western Europe is also pushing away from economic and political domination by the United States of America.

This new nationalism has wrought momentous changes. It is changing the post-war alliances within both the Communist and non-Communist world. It presents great difficulties for the United Nations and the ideas of world federation and Atlantic union.

By fostering national barriers, the new nationalism in one sense obstructs international cooperation. Paradoxically, by reducing ideological barriers, this new nationalism in another sense permits greater international cooperation based on the principle of equality of nations. In October, 1961, when the White House was divided on whether to support the fledgling European Economic Community, or whether to request a year's extension of the Reciprocal Trade Agreements Act, I urged support of the E. E. C. as the most realistic step toward economic and political stability, and hence world peace. Why? Because the E. E. C. was founded on the simple principle of removing nationalistic barriers to international trade.

The principle of a high protective tariff is basic to a government-protected, or owned, or managed economy. High tariffs inhibit cross-cultural relations. Freer trade, on the other hand, enables the peoples of different nations to become better acquainted with the customs, beliefs, ways of life, and government policies of one another. With the greater expansion and ease of communication today, freer trade induces mutual international understanding.

When international understanding is thus achieved, political tensions are reduced and voices of reason are easier heard and understood. The way is then prepared to move toward world stability, increased prosperity, higher standards of living and education, and peaceful competitive existence in international markets. These conditions, in turn, form the foundation for cooperative political policies among nations.

Two and one-half years of bargaining within the European Economic Community are coming to a close with expectation of the most substantial tariff reductions in history. The effects of this action will spread all over the world—from Europe to Latin America, Africa, and Asia. I quote from a recent statement by the Japanese Ambassador: "We Japanese believe that contacts through trade tend to facilitate mutual understanding among nations of differing ideologies and social structures."

This development is not as dramatic and grandiose as a League of Nations, a United Nations, or world law based on a world court. However, international trade is the only proven method for initiating a workable peace with international security and understanding— security and understanding that might save the United Nations organization which is now bankrupt financially, politically, and structurally. The world needs the United Nations as a forum to discuss and expose international grievances and concerns.

Early in 1966, our President requested Congress to repeal legislation obstructing United States trade with Communist countries. Congress adjourned without acting on the President's trade recommendations. Meanwhile, the English, French, West Germans, and Japanese are filling the orders of China, the Soviet Union, and Eastern Europe. Our allies are trading with Communist countries. We are not.

The defensive "white elephant" military structures of SEATO and CENTO exist only on paper. Despite our rebuilding efforts, NATO's days are numbered. These alliances were not designed to provide the common ground for better acquaintance with, and understanding of, the Communist world. Nevertheless, our own nationalism persists to inhibit the expansion of

America's world trade. The American Congress has not learned a prime lesson of history—that economic isolationism leads to political isolationism as well as the converse, and that either is counter-productive in this day and age, as even the Soviet Union is reluctantly learning.

The world is truly in an era of greatest change. World peace and stability depend on harmonious relations between China, the Soviet Union, and the United States. The time has come for each to completely reappraise its foreign policies. Each major power must ask itself whether it correctly perceives new realities, whether momentous world changes have evoked commensurate policy responses. Specifically, each must introspectively assess whether continuing confrontation with its military strength is the most effective means to assure world peace and stability and hence its own security.

What are these new realities? They include: the Soviet modernizing of Communist dogma, the Sino-Soviet split, European self-determination and independence from Soviet and American domination, the advent of Chinese nuclear power, the growing non-alignment of developing nations, the recession of the Communist tide, and worldwide acceptance of the concept of the welfare state. In a nut shell, these are the new challenges wrought by the new nationalism.

The potential colossus of China, weakened internally and externally by Mao's unrealistic fanatic militancy, bitterly attacks both the Soviet Union and the United States. The irony is that these attacks help to induce better relations between these super powers—exactly what China fears.

The Soviet Union faces hostility from China on her eastern front—the closest and most obvious mark for its new nuclear bomb—with the longest border line in the world, and territorial disputes and memories of bloody invasions centuries old. The passage of time has not eliminated from the folklore of Russian memories the ravages of Genghis Khan's hordes, or Napoleon's French, or German armies twice in the last fifty years. It was Mao's leadership that chased Russia out of Manchuria.

On her western front, the Soviet Union fears a united Germany as the devil fears holy water. In all of Russian history, there has been one basic foreign policy and that is to avoid facing a war at the same time on two fronts.

By the same token, China—without a navy—faces the United States of America on her Pacific front and the Soviet Union on her land front.

Both the Soviet Union and China face the United States of America uncertain as to the international policies of the greatest economic power, welfare state, and military power in the world. The Soviet lately links together both China and the United States of America in formal public attacks. The corollary of such attacks is what the Soviet fears.

We have this definite situation that the Soviet Union needs the pressure of America in the Pacific, despite Premier Kosygin's continued assertions that ". . . if the war [in Vietnam] were ended, relations [with America] would certainly improve." China, in turn, needs the pressure of America in Europe on the Soviet Union, despite Mao's attacks on both. The peace of the world is in suspense while this jockeying goes on.

Hence, America is presented with an unusual opportunity to initiate a "live-and-let-live" policy of competitive economic existence with the Soviet Union, or China, or preferably both. Such American initiatives are necessary to reduce tensions, violence, war, and threats of war, in other words — to normalize international relations. Encouragingly, these policies seem to be developing.

In 1966, President Johnson made three highly significant foreign policy moves that have generally escaped the public attention and discussion they deserve, and have yet to be explained to the American people. Foremost among the foreign policies of the Truman, Eisenhower, Kennedy, and Johnson administrations were the reunification of Germany and the political and economic isolation of Communist China. These two policies, together with the implications of the President's commitments at the Manila Conference, signify possibly momentous changes in our foreign policy.

The first of these three significant moves by President Johnson occurred in July, 1966, when he proposed at least a tentative reappraisal of our China policy with his offer of reconciliation with China. I quote President Johnson: "Lasting peace can never come to Asia as long as the 700 million people of mainland China are isolated by their rulers from the outside world.

"We persist [in efforts to improve relations] because we believe that cooperation, not hostility, is the way of the future. That day is not here yet. It may be long in coming, but it is clearly on the way, and come it must."

In September, 1966, Vice-president Humphrey followed President Johnson's incipient design by speaking of "building bridges to China." I have been urging such a policy for a long time, but without success. Recently, spokesmen for the United States Chamber of Commerce are on record as stating that increased communication with the Peking government is in order. And, according to a recent report of the American Friends Service Committee, our present policy of non-intercourse with China is leading to disaster. Said the Committee, and I quote: "Two of the largest and most powerful nations of the world have since 1950 lived largely in isolated ignorance of one another and in an atmosphere of mutual fear and hate. . . . Some attempt to break the present deadlock is long and dangerously overdue."

The point to be emphasized here is not that our China policy is soon to be reversed. China has replied to the President with more lies and abuse. Rather, the question of great interest to both the United States and the Soviet Union is—After Mao, what? It is in anticipation of answering this important question that the pending reappraisal of our China policy acquires added significance.

The second of the three meaningful moves was inherent in Mr. Johnson's assertion of August 1966 that better relations with the Soviet Union "must be our first concern." By implication, the President thereby signaled our intention to abandon the priority of the reunification of Germany. I quote from Joseph C. Harsch in the *Christian Science Monitor*: ". . . the President has formally stated that reunification of Germany can come about only within the reunification of Europe. Germany's cause is no longer Step One in healing the split in Europe caused by the cold war. The unity of Germany is a hoped-for result of closer East-West ties. It is no longer the precondition."

Two recent developments in Germany might possibly be related. They are: (1) The downfall of the Erhard government replaced by an uncertain coalition of the Christian Democrats and the Social Democrats; and (2) a resurgence of German nationalism as evidenced in state legislative elections.

A *quid pro quo* for this momentous change in our European policy could be for the Soviet Union to use its good offices in bringing about a settlement in Vietnam that would be worthy of our sacrifice of blood and money. An end to the Vietnam war, according to Premier Kosygin, would pave the way to improved relations. Recently he said, "We want a relaxation of tension; we want an understanding with the United States."

The Soviet Union would have much to gain. She would be free of a threat on her western front which would allow her to concentrate on the growing Chinese military threat on her long eastern front.

The third and last move fraught with momentous consequences for all the world concerns President Johnson's pre-election Manila Conference. I quote from a report by the Research Institute:

First the Conference left untouched the one crucial issue: Where does the Vietcong figure in the war's final settlement? South Viet Premier Ky made clear where he figures the Vietcong: destroyed as an organization, its members "abiding by the law"—the South Vietnam law as enforced by the government headed by Ky.

It is inconceivable that Hanoi or the Vietcong will negotiate on any such terms, unless Ky should retract his words publicly. It is equally inconceivable that he will yield on any of them.

The stage is set, hence, for a long drawn-out tug-of-war among the Manila conferees—with no end to the fighting itself. The allied stalemate may be harder to break than the field impasse.

And concluding from this report:

If Ky were alone, he might be brought to heel fairly soon. But he has real support from the South Koreans, Thais and Australians. They do not want to see the Vietcong in a peacetime Saigon government either; they are in this to stop Red expansion, no matter what it takes.

This is different from what the Filipinos, New Zealand—and the United States—are ready to accept: Let the Vietcong into the government. Philippine President Marcos is ambitious to become Asia's peacemaker even at the cost of including the VC.

This is the United States position, as well, although President Johnson did not press it openly at Manilia.

The Manila Conference was a complete failure as far as agreement on any Vietnam peace settlement is concerned. Before the ink was dry, Premier Ky of South Vietnam emphatically dissented from President Johnson's interpretation of the Manila Conference proceedings, just as he did with President Johnson's interpretation of the so-called Honolulu Pact. Again I quote from the Research Institute report: "After Manila . . . Ky has only one clear course left: Keep the U. S. fighting until the Vietcong has been totally smashed. This means more men and arms, more escalation, a much wider war."

It should also be noted that the much heralded free election law in that unhappy country gives Ky and his military junta a veto over any measure the civilian assembly adopts.

One result of the Manila Conference was the dramatic pronouncement by our President that the United States is a major Asian power and is assuming guardianship in its name over all of Asia. This appears to be an assertion of national responsibility of appalling proportions. Should Congress implement Johnson's Asian manifesto, it would seem that America would become permanently and deeply involved—politically, militarily, economically—in all Asia.

Many months have passed without any explanation by our President of his sweeping pronouncement. Why is the President silent? Americans are kept in the dark as to just what was said at Manila by our President— and what his intentions are.

Of equal present and future importance is how other governments interpret President Johnson's Manila manifesto. Do they consider it as a definite projection of U. S. foreign policy? Or do they consider his expansive statement as merely a gesture of good intentions designed to obscure the utter failure of the Conference to agree on peace in Vietnam? Have they learned that American presidents' words do not "always weigh a ton"—as Mr. Coolidge said?

Perhaps, when interpreting our President's Manila statement, other governments might recall previous American international commitments which we did not honor—as, for example, the Open Door for China which we ignored when Japan invaded Manchuria in 1931. Or they might recall the Buffalo speech of John Foster Dulles during the 1952 presidential election campaign pledging the new administration—if elected—to liberation of the captive nations of Eastern Europe—a pledge that was to contribute to the Hungarian revolt of 1956 in expectation of American support that was never forthcoming.

Or, our President's Manila pronouncement might be explained as "speaking softly but carrying a big stick." If this is the correct interpretation, then the question must be asked—just how big a stick does America intend to carry in Asia in the light of spreading nuclear power? Do we really need such paramountcy in Asia?

In October, 1964, China formally proposed a conference of the five nuclear powers preliminary to a conference of all nations to abolish nuclear weapons. I immediately urged American acceptance at least for the purpose of discussion. Secretary General U Thant somewhat unprecedentedly publicly endorsed my statement the next morning. But the Johnson administration dismissed offhand China's overture, on the ground that it was mere propaganda, that China's nuclear bomb was obsolete, and that it would be twenty or more years before China would perfect the means of delivering it. But, in less than two years, China demonstrated that it had already achieved the capacity to develop an on-target missile delivery system and a bomb with thermonuclear characteristics.

Finally, there is the question—if President Johnson meant what he seemed to say at Manila—where is he

ALFRED M. LANDON

going to get the money to bring his Great Society to all of Asia? And this in addition to the pressing question of where is he going to get the money to finance both a big war and yet continue his Great Society for the home folks?

If our President's new Asian policy is undertaken, the greater question must be asked: What responsibility—moral or otherwise—do we Americans actually have to bankrupt ourselves for President Johnson's unrealistic policy for world salvation?

If this policy is described as a part of the program to contain Communism, let us observe how Communism is containing itself by its unworkable theories, as can be seen in Communist dominated countries everywhere. Indonesia is the latest example, plus a number of African states that have kicked out both Chinese and Russian attempts at Communist domination.

It will be the responsibility of our Congress to implement President Johnson's Manila manifesto, or to refuse to assume its frightful consequences, when and if the President requests the necessary appropriations to implement it. Even a token Congressional appropriation would be tantamount to the assumption of responsibility that would lead to various future complications.

While the President's astounding Manila manifesto does not require treaty ratification by the United States Senate, it is so vital to American interests that I believe that the Senate Foreign Relations Committee ought to probe all its facets and to expose all its implications, and our obligations under it, for the attention of the American people as well as peoples elsewhere.

There must be a clear and complete understanding not only between the American people and their government, but also among the governments that participated at Manila as to what exactly are we Americans expected to do for our Asian wards, what specific commitments and limitations were made by President Johnson, and how lasting will they be. For some unknown reason, President Johnson has chosen not to discuss these great concerns with the American people. Meanwhile, other governments should clearly understand that President Johnson's exuberant Asian commitments require Congressional action under our system to become operative.

The simplest way to clear this all up is to get the complete transcript of the Manila Conference before the Senate Foreign Relations Committee for introduction in the *Congressional Record*.

There remains one other critical development that threatens to enlarge even further the stretching world commitments of the United States. I speak of the growing pressures to impose economic embargoes through the United Nations on Rhodesia and the Republic of South Africa. To enforce its decision to end the South African mandate over Southwest Africa, the United Nations may soon impose economic sanctions on South Africa, as well as Rhodesia.

When Britian attempted to bring Rhodesia to heel by imposing sanctions, President Johnson promptly concurred. But these sanctions have failed. Now Prime Minister Wilson is apparently caught bluffing again. When his bold words in his report to the British Parliament of his conference with the Prime Minister of Rhodesia are boiled down, they are nothing but the same old appeal for "special sanctions" by the United Nations on purchases of key Rhodesian products.

From the beginning, it has been evident that Prime Minister Wilson is trying to bluff Rhodesia back into line by threats.

If the United Nations adopts a more forcible policy, who is going to enforce it?

I quote from John Knight's "Editor's Scrapbook":

> Mr. Wilson would like nothing more than to have the United States pull his chestnuts out of the fire. As the *Economist* of London has said: "To pretend that Britain alone can resolve this problem is just as stupid as to think it can be handed over to the U. N. That duty (sanctions) does not rest with the British government alone. The cloud in Mr. Ian Smith's sky may seem no bigger than a man's hand; but the real question is whether the hand is President Johnson's."

> And the *London Sunday Observer* comments that it must be up to the United States to make effective the sanctions on Rhodesia, the Republic of South Africa and Southwest Africa.

The only effective means of enforcing economic embargoes is by naval blockade, not to mention air cover. To effectively blockade the coast of South and Southwest Africa would be a prodigious and very expensive undertaking. Our navy is already fully committed. Our First Fleet is patrolling the California coast, and the Second Fleet the Atlantic coast. Our Sixth Fleet operates in the Mediterranean area, and our Seventh Fleet in the straits between Taiwan and China and the rest of the Pacific area, including South Vietnam.

Any effective embargo of Rhodesia would require

a blockade of South Africa. The volume of South African trade alone with Great Britain might well involve the solvency of the British pound.

How can we support the solvency of the British pound and yet enforce such economic embargoes on Rhodesia or South Africa, or both, and yet fight a major war in South Vietnam, not to mention all the other American commitments at home and abroad?

This African affair will not be settled in one week or one month. It can be as long as the engagement in Vietnam.

From every side, then, there is a pressing need for the Senate Foreign Relations Committee to review and assess the position America occupies as the result of its exuberant evangelical world leadership in Europe, in Asia, in Africa, and in this hemisphere.

While I staunchly believe in and support President Johnson's policies of new contacts with both the Soviet Union and China as the basis for better international understanding, I believe Senator Fulbright's announced plan for a full and comprehensive review by the Senate Foreign Relations Committee in both public and closed hearings is both timely and essential.

Long ago, I said the United Nations could not succeed in its objectives if it left out Communist China.

President Johnson has taken the first steps with both China and the Soviet Union. There has been no commensurate response from either.

Our President is leading from strength, both economically and militarily. There is as much need—perhaps more—for our national administration's intelligent concentration on strengthening our economic foundations and backlogs as its concentration on strengthening our military.

It is now up to the Soviet Union to demonstrate the change of front—that Premier Kosygin desires—by performance rather than by words. After all, credibility is as essential in political relations as it is in trade.

Let me conclude by saying simply this: We should respond to the new nationalism and other new challenges in international relations in our continuing search for world peace. I believe we are on the threshold of abandoning our foolish and unrealistic China policy. At the same time, we are hopefully making progress toward improving relations with East European nations.

Now, at last, a realistic basis exists for discussions between the Soviet Union and the United States of a new policy for both countries.

Should China recover from her present insanity and join in responsible interaction with the Soviet Union and the United States—a new era in international relations would commence that would shape the destiny of this world by creating stability on which peace with security is ultimately based. This must be our hope. This must be our aim.

The Emerging South: Politics and Issues

Ralph McGill

I AM greatly complimented to be one of those invited to participate in the lecture series that bears the name of and honors the man Alfred Landon. He has lived—and continues to live—a life of usefulness and of excellence. He has made—and still makes—a contribution to our life and times that has been critically constructive. His participation in the national dialogue has been—and is—one that properly commands respect and appreciation.

My pleasure at being here and attempting to discuss something of the political development of the Southeastern United States—that controversial region known generally as "the South"—is increased because this same Alfred Landon was responsible for inspiring me to try to do something about it.

Some months after the presidential campaign of 1936, I was on a visit to Washington for my paper. Mr. Landon happened also to be there. He was gracious enough to see a newspaperman unknown to him. We talked about the lamentable condition of party politics in the South. I raised in particular the low estate of what was then known as the Republican Party in the states of the old Confederacy. It was, in a sense, a non-existent party. Its members were contemptuously known as the "Post Office" Republicans. They were a few men who handled the post office and other patronage appointments when a Republican was elected President. These men also controlled the selection of delegates to the national conventions. In between, most of them made common cause with state Democratic factions and, at the county level, functioned as Democrats.

Mark Hanna of Ohio, maker of the Republican Party, is credited with establishing this skeleton-like organization. Some months before the national convention that nominated William McKinley, Mr. Hanna appeared in the then small town of Thomasville, Georgia, just north of the Florida line. A house had been rented for him. Mr. Hanna announced, to the great satisfaction of local pride, that he had come to Thomasville for his health. It was noted, however, that a surprising number of persons became interested in Mr. Hanna's health. Callers came every day. They came by train and carriage. Most of them stayed at the local hotels, except an occasional one or two who were guests at the Hanna home.

Mr. Hanna was practicing one of the arts of king-making. He had earlier determined to nominate Mr.

McKinley on the first ballot. It occurred to him that while there was no Republican Party in Dixie, there were delegates. Before he reached Thomasville and took a house, letters and a few telephone calls had alerted persons in all the states of the Deep South to be ready to go to Thomasville and ask about Mr. Hanna's health. Mr. Hanna's health improved with each visiting delegation. When he returned home to Ohio he was interviewed about his health and that of the Republican Party. He said both were good. Indeed, he predicted that Mr. McKinley would be nominated on the first ballot. He was. He had a significant majority and a substantial portion of it was a solid block of votes by delegations from the Southern states. It was merely coincidental that chairmen who answered the roll call of these Southern states were all men who had been to Thomasville to inquire about Mr. Hanna's health. From that time until 1952 Southern delegations traditionally were tied by influence to leadership from Ohio. They were counted in the Taft corner for President William Howard Taft and they were later supporters of the presidential ambitions of Senator Robert Taft.

Indeed, it was a part of the political irony of our times that the nomination of General Dwight Eisenhower at the 1952 convention turned on a pivot of a Southern state—Georgia—and a contest of the seating of the delegation. The old line Post Office Republicans had controlled the state convention and had ruled out delegates committed to General Eisenhower's candidacy. Two delegations showed up at the Republican convention of that year. The convention's credentials committee seated the Taft delegation. A contest from the floor followed. In a rare and historic decision the delegates reversed the convention's credentials committee and seated the delegation committed to General Eisenhower. This precedent was followed by a similar decision regarding contesting delegations from Texas, and within minutes, the stampede to General Eisenhower was on. I recall sitting in the press section during that decision and having Mrs. Oveta Culp Hobby say to me, "Who would ever have expected a Republican convention to turn on the state of Georgia and on a moral issue at that?"

Governor Landon and I had talked in 1937. At that time he discussed, among other things, the quality of Republican delegations from the South. His conclusion was that they were, on the whole, a rather second-rate lot. There were individual exceptions, but in the main, these delegations were made up largely of men who, the Governor said, would not be admitted to state Republican delegations from other sections of the country. In this he was entirely correct. They were a second-rate lot and some of them were third- and fourth-rate. This was well known locally, but the Republican Party also was known locally not to be a party in fact, but merely a skeleton-type organization which made no effort to build a party organization at either the local or state level. Governor Landon further concluded that not until the Republican National Committee was willing to give assistance and consideration to responsible Southerners would there be a development of the two-party system in the South.

I printed this interview and it created a mild and temporary tempest. Two or three of the local Republican leaders issued indignant denials, but they soon subsided in the face of the undeniable facts of what Governor Landon had said.

There is today the beginnings of a two-party system in the South. The Republican Party as it exists is neither a united nor a happy one. Its leadership is all too often those who have deserted the Democratic Party because of opposition to civil rights legislation. Too much of the Republican effort in the South has been, and is, an attempt to win votes by adopting programs more racist than those of the Southern Democrats. It cannot be said that a single state Republican organization in the South has endorsed the Republican national platform planks on civil rights. In 1964, for example, Governor George Wallace of Alabama gave aid and comfort to a number of Republican candidates for Congress and for other local offices. Republican election gains were significant insofar as the labels meant anything. Republicans won victories. But in 1966 Governor Wallace turned against these same men when he determined to support a slate of state nominees who would be favorable to his wife's candidacy for the governor and to his later third party "Southern Democratic" movement. The Republicans in Alabama, therefore, bit the dust.

In 1966 there was a general falling-off of Southern Republican successes as compared with those in 1964. Senator Goldwater's political managers had determined on what they called the "Southern strategy." This was, in reality, a poorly concealed racist strategy. It was based on the belief that Senator Goldwater could not win the Northern Negro vote. They felt that he might conceivably carry some of the Northern states, but they believed he would, by satisfying Southern racists, gather in the whole bloc of Southern electoral votes and perhaps win in the electoral college.

In Georgia, in 1964, the present Governor, Mr. Lester Maddox, then engaged in an open running fight against public accommodation laws, cynically declared that Senator Goldwater's racial position suited him (Mr. Maddox). In Alabama, George Wallace abandoned his own third party racist program so that he would not get in Senator Goldwater's way.

This racist dilemma will continue to plague the Southern Republican development, but as I see it, it is, while sad and regrettable, perhaps a necessary part of the trauma of developing a second party. Nor should the melodrama of race by the so-called Southern Republicans hide the fact that there are many reputable first rate men who are at work trying to create a Southern Republican Party of responsibility and prestige. Some of these men had managed to make considerable progress until the take-over by Goldwater forces in 1964. They were not, and are not, racists. They are men committed to what they believe to be the principles of a progressive conservation. Most of them were replaced as state chairmen and national committeemen by the Goldwater organizational take-over in 1964, but they are coming back. They are by no means lost to the struggle to create a responsible competing party.

The Southern Democrats are not without trauma and dilemma. The divisive effects of racism and the determination of rural leaders to maintain segregated school systems at no matter what the cost to educational standards in general have contributed to a substantial split in what used to be called the solid Democratic South. We now know that in fact we had no Democratic Party such as existed in states outside the South. In the Southern one-party states the Democratic Party was what the governor made it. There were factions, each calling itself Democrats, that contended for the governorship.

When in 1964 and 1966 it became necessary for Southern Democrats to function as a party, they found themselves without any efficient, effective state organizations. They had never needed such organizations, because there had been an absence of opposition. They found their own ranks split by racist divisions. There is increasing disposition on the part of young voters not necessarily to follow the party of their fathers, but to split their votes and act more and more as independent voters, rather than those with party affiliation. It cannot now be said that the Democratic Party in the South is well organized or that it will be so in time for the 1968 campaign. Certainly racist influences will plague and embarrass both parties in the next presidential campaign.

I believe it necessary that there be a greater national comprehension of the political and social history of the South, because the effects of that history are now, in truth, a national problem, political, economic and social. Let me say, further, that it is not my purpose to berate the South. It is my region. I was born in it. I have lived and worked in it. But the romanticized myth of the South has been, and is, a curse to those who live there. The myth still obscures the reality.

The creation of a system of segregation was an evil, the effects of which were deep and widespread beyond the easy assumption that it merely separated the races in travel, in education, and in housing. It subjected the Negro to a separation that made it impossible for him to know anything of participation in citizenship, much less the responsibilities of it. Segregation gave to the white Southerner a false sense of position and values. In trying to pay for two school systems with a per capita income that was inadequate to finance one good school system, he subjected all children to an education inferior to that provided children of other regions. He slowed the industrial development of his region. He delayed the appearance of managerial skills and the accumulation of capital. There was also the profound moral dilemma of always justifying and supporting an immoral system.

Political maturity was impossible under that system. It was, for example, not really possible for a second party to develop in the South until 1958 when the U. S. Supreme Court ruled the white primary unconstitutional. The white primary device was one that restricted the voters to white persons. There was no opposition party. The primary was the election. The white primary and the poll tax created political apathy among white persons. Today the percentage of Southerners who vote is well below the national average.

The white power structure that created the device restricting the ballot wanted to attain that result—a general lack of voter participation.

In Missisippi, in 1900, it openly was argued that "the poll tax gets rid of most of the Negroes and also gets rid of a great many undesirable whites at the same time."

In 1901 Henry Fontaine Reese, of Selma and Dallas County (Alabama), stood before the state legislative convention and appealed for a constitutional poll tax provision.

"When you pay $1.50 for a poll tax in Dallas County, I believe you disfranchise 10 Negroes," he said. "Give us this $1.50 for educational purposes and for disfranchisement of a vicious and useless class.

"There has been talk," said delegate Reese, "from the hills of north Alabama as to what the poor white boys want. I do not propose to put my people under the hand of Negro rule because it might disfranchise one or two bastards in the white counties of Alabama."

Participation in the fraud, admitted cheating, and dishonesty of the disfranchisement proceedings had an effect on what the late W. J. Cash called "The Mind of the South." A large majority of poor white persons were delivered, along with almost all Negroes, into the political control of a minority of white voters.

All this chicanery had to be justified. Out of it came the doctrines of white supremacy, of Negro inferiority, and a system of segregation whose moral, political, social and economic injustices, follies, and evils are just now being comprehended.

What is not fully comprehended is that the product of the South's evil of segregation with all its ramifications deprived not merely a top-heavy majority of the nation's Negroes, but also hundreds of thousands of white children of education and citizenship. This product has now been exported to all the nation. It is a part of the complexity of life and government in Kansas City, in

Topeka, in Seattle, in Miami—in all the cities of the nation.

An immense migration out of the rural South and the Southwest began in the decade of the boll weevil in 1920-30. It slowed during the depression, but it became accelerated as the nation moved into the Second World War, and it has not stopped. The peak area of migration was in the decades of 1940-1950 and 1950-1960. Not all of this has been Negro. A substantial percentage has been poor white farmers, tenants, or croppers who are no longer needed on the land. But most of them have been Negro.

San Francisco will do as an example. This beautiful and historic city has always had a cosmopolitan population. In 1940 the Negro population in San Francisco was a little over 5,000. But in 1941 Japan practically wiped out our Pacific fleet. It became necessary to re-take the Pacific. To do this, we had to build some 60,000 aircraft, ships, landing craft, and weapons of all sizes. War plants from Seattle to San Diego filled up with workers, most of them off the farms of Southern states—Oklahoma, Texas, and other agricultural states. In 1945 San Francisco's Negro population was 50,000.

Americans could better understand the discontent and the spontaneity of slum violence in the larger cities if they knew the background. In the span of time between 1940-1963, almost 3½ million Negroes left the South. The war-time shipyards, aviation, and other war plants were the magnets that accelerated this out-migration. Out-migration continued after this peak period as farm machines replaced human beings and mules. An official estimate reveals that 114,000 Negroes left 11 counties in Mississippi in the recent decade of 1950-1960. Two and a half million Negroes have left the South since 1960. The out movement has slowed for obvious reasons, but it continues. The condition of the farm population in the old cotton states will worsen in the years ahead.

Early in 1967 a U. S. Senate sub-committee, composed of respected Republicans and Democrats, made public the results of personal investigation and the taking of evidence in Mississippi. It was a shocking report on the poverty of rural persons, mostly in the South, who are no longer needed on the land.

An estimated 15 million of over 38 million poor are rural Americans. Half the nation's farm-operator families have incomes less than $3,000. At least 500,000 rural families whose chief income is farm wages live well below the poverty lovel.

Conditions are even worse for the five million rural Negroes. More than half have incomes of less than $2,000. In fact, perhaps a third have cash returns below $500 or less per year.

Urban poverty may, after all, be seen if one persists and goes out of the way to look for it. But rural misery is, on the whole, rather scattered and more hidden. It is, therefore, even more neglected, demonstrating the truth of the axiom, "out of sight, out of mind."

The Senate sub-committee found shameful exploitation of the food stamp program. It recommended a careful, studied reform of the welfare program. We will, I think, ignore this report to our peril.

There is, of course, a chorus of grumbling about

poverty programs and loud denunciation of recipients as "not working." The comparison is not exact, to be sure, but we do not become exasperated because the many years of experimenting with cancer research has not produced a cure. Generations passed before the scourge of tuberculosis was brought under control. Poverty is more costly and dangerous than cancer or any other disease. It produces, of course, its own by-product of disease and crime.

There is a long hot summer ahead. It is, indeed, almost at hand. The tensions resulting from the exporting from farms to cities of millions of poor, unskilled, illiterate and semi-literate persons across the last four decades; the huge increase in population, half of which is 25 years old or younger—plus the burdens of war— have increased and added complexity to our lives.

It is a part of the problem that our heavy increase in population corresponded roughly with the out-migration from the South and the rural areas generally. The Census Bureau tells us that about 100 million of our 200 million population are 25 years old and younger. Everything is crowded—campuses, cities, suburbs.

We will be further tested, regionally and nationally, by riots, draft-card burners, imitators of Cassius Clay, and activities of the extremists of what is collectively called the New Left.

The New Left in America is not numerically strong. It is itself somewhat fragmented. It has, within the context of its far-out position, its own extremists advocating violence and also elements not yet fully committed to programs of anarchy. There are some who are training "urban guerrillas" to fight police and other law enforcement representatives from cellars, alley ways, and hidden positions. There are others that plan protests, riots, and related tactics.

They can succeed only if Americans lose a sense of balance and act out of anger and emotional impulses. It is difficult to put down reactions to those who burn or degrade the nation's flag, who do lead Hanoi to think it can win the war in America, or who lend themselves to the more irrational forms of protest. But it is precisely this weakness in human nature that is relied upon by the extreme of the New Left. They know they, few in number, can succeed only if they arouse a massive social and political swing to the "right." Hence, we may expect to be subjected to continued irritations and provocations—all aimed at upsetting the national balance and purpose. The provocateurs want to demoralize the society they have come to hate. They will keep trying to prod us to abandon the basic strengths of our society to retaliate against them.

Congressman Hebert's outburst against one of the deliberately staged provocations, an insult to the flag, was to suggest that we "forget about the first amendment and jail those who seek to destroy our society but seek protection of its laws."

This, of course, plays into the hands of the provocateurs. The Congressman spoke spontaneously in indignation. If we are provoked into selective "forgetting" of any of the foundations on which our form of government is established, then these foundations will in time disappear by becoming meaningless.

The New Left is estimated to include about 200,000 persons. Its more extreme members, willing to use repeated irrational violence to bring on chaos and, hopefully, a condition of anarchy, cannot succeed, either on the campuses or in the city slums, unless Americans succumb to emotional, angry retaliations as excessive as the provocations and, thereby, themselves contribute to a sense and a presence of anarchy.

The New Left, including, as it does, adults who join in the acts of wholly irrational protests and demonstrations, already has had a considerable success. They have helped create an impulsive, blind reaction that has enabled reactionary forces in and out of the Congress to slow, or halt, the necessary and hopeful progress of recent years.

The spectacle of some of the one-time personalities in social progress turning to "peace protests" because today "peace is where the money is" is a further aid to the forces of reaction and, therefore, indirectly to the worst of the New Left.

There are 38 million Americans whose critical conditions of poverty are undenied. There are massive, shocking gaps in the education provided the poor and the children of the middle and upper income groups. There are millions of Americans, exiles from agriculture, particularly Southern agriculture, who are crowded into slum areas of cities. There is, in this nation, almost no housing for the very poor. The very poor include hundreds of thousands of Spanish-speaking have-nots and hundreds of thousands of "poor whites" from Appalachia and the obsolete small farms.

The young Negro in the South is aware of the progress made. But he still finds himself in predominately or all-Negro state schools and colleges which he knows to be second- and third-rate. He is aware of the injustice of the past and the slow pace of the present. This is why some of them listen to the Stokely Carmichaels. One can easily imagine the frustration, despair, and emotional tensions of a young Negro in states governed by a George Wallace, a Lester Maddox, or others like them whose commitments have been to rigid segregation and an inferior citizenship for the Negro.

It should be obvious that the immediate and long-time needs of 38 million Americans should not be abandoned because of the often stupid, reckless, irrational protests and deliberately provocative acts of such governors as are symbolized by Wallace and Maddox or by those of the New Left who are hostile to the existing society. The racists benefit by neglect of the needs of the deprived American. The New Left also is aided and encouraged, and the cure of our most dangerous and damaging ills is unnecessarily delayed.

Jefferson believed that if the people could be helped to know and comprehend the facts, they would, in the end, act with common sense. We are in a period, complex, emotional, and difficult, when common sense, understanding, and patience are required of us.

Higher Education: Its Role in Contemporary America

Ronald Reagan

I AM speaking here today neither as an academician nor as a politician. I do not have the training to be the first nor the aspiration to be the second. That leaves me the role of concerned citizen, and among my concerns is higher education and its place in contemporary America.

Listing the problems is easy—solutions are a little harder to come by. For example, there is the problem of financing the increasing cost of higher education. I have some first-hand experience with that one, but I cannot lay claim to having the answer. Nor do I think that university president has the answer who stated bluntly that the academic community's only responsibility was to tell government its needs, and government's obligation was not to question but to simply come up with the money. This was higher education and contemporary America meeting eyeball to eyeball.

Strange as it may seem, there is a limit to what government can extract from the body of the citizenry—a limit fixed, not by pity or unwillingness to wield the scalpel, but by the hard fact that unless that body of citizenry is able to function on a 9-to-5 basis, the schoolhouse door will not open at all.

Government's share of the wealth has to stop short of interfering with the production of wealth. Higher education explains it as having to do with the law of diminishing returns.

Then, of course, having decided on and collected its share, government must allocate. So much for roads —so much for protection against the lawbreaker—for help to those who must depend on the rest of us for sustenance—for health—and, of course, for education, elementary through college and university.

Never, according to those engaged in these various facets of government, is there sufficient funding for all that needs to be done. But when government is taking all the economy will bear, choices must be made, and, if education demands an increase in funds greater than the normal workload increase occasioned by growth and higher prices, then it must be taken from some other program.

Now this should not be interpreted as minimizing the importance of education. No one denies the value of a higher education for all those able to assimilate one. Indeed, a vast network of institutions of higher learning, both public and private, is essential if we are to maintain our nation as the world's leader in science and technology. Nor does anyone deny the growing needs in our nation for teachers, for doctors, lawyers, economists, and sociologists, and yes in these days, not only for a literate public, but also for a well-educated and knowledgeable populace.

Alfred Whitehead said, "In the conditions of modern life, the rule is absolute: The race which does not value trained intelligence is doomed."

There is no question but that Americans all over this land have assigned a high priority to education. It is also true that the cost of education is increasing faster than the increase in public funds. A more sophisticated answer is needed than just "come up with more money."

I suggested a partial answer in California based on the theory that good tax policy involves assessing at least a part of the charge for a service against those receiving the service. In a word, I proposed tuition at our state university and colleges. The result was cataclysmic. I could not have branded myself as any more "anti-intellectual" if I had said, "Me Tarzan, you Jane." Actually, there was much more to my proposal than just a method for collecting revenue.

The students enjoying the benefits of public higher education in California came from the same income levels as those attending the private or independent schools such as Stanford and U. S. C. Very few from low income families can take advantage of the educational opportunities made available by the taxpayers of California. With this in mind, half of the funds from the proposed tuition would go for a combination of loans and grants-in-aid to needy students.

RONALD REAGAN
109

And since another problem in our university is an exceptionally high dropout rate, we tried to cope with that. Our plan called for 75 per cent loan and 25 per cent grant the first year, 50-50 the second year, 75 per cent grant and only 25 per cent loan the third year, and 100 per cent grant the fourth year. The loans, of course, would be repaid after graduation.

Another problem at our university is the unhappiness of students over lack of contact with professors engaged more in research than in teaching. To help meet this problem, one-fourth of the tuition money would provide for 250 new teaching chairs at the university and the remaining fourth could be applied to capital construction of needed facilities.

Since all of this could be accomplished with a tuition that amounted to less than 10 per cent of the cost of the education, we did not think the proposal was punitive.

May I add that, if we adhere to the idea that everything adds to the educational experience, I believe there is some merit in the student accepting responsibility for a portion of the cost of his education —as long as no qualified student is denied an education because of lack of funds.

There are benefits and burdens that accrue both to the individual and to society, and the burdens, including the burden of cost, must be borne by both.

But if all the problems of finance could be solved tomorrow, there would still be cause for concern about the place of higher education in contemporary America.

What is our definition of academic freedom? Those who teach, understandably enough, define it as the right to teach as they see fit without interference from administrators and certainly not from those who hold the public purse strings or who fill the public purse. But those who pay for the education, students and taxpayers, also have a definition of academic freedom: Their freedom to have some say in what they get for their money.

Those holding public office try to interpret the will of the people and pass it on to the university administration, conscious always that they must not appear to be exerting political control over education. Equally uncomfortable are the administrators who must interpret the educators' viewpoint to the crass politicians and vice versa—they can be likened to a prisoner in front of a cellophane wall being shouted at by both sides.

And the truth is—all the claims are legitimate and must be reconciled within a framework of mutual understanding and compromise.

The dictionary defines education as "the impartation or acquisition of knowledge, skill, or the development of character as by study or discipline."

The taxpayer is wrong who ignores the great increase in things we know—knowledge acquired since he was in school—and who demands "no new-fangled courses. What was good enough then is good enough now." But so is the student wrong who would eliminate all required courses and grades—who would make education a kind of four-year smorgasbord in which he would be the sole judge of how far and fast he ran in pursuit of knowledge. And that educator is wrong who denies there are any absolutes—who sees no black and white of right or wrong, but just shades of gray in a world where discipline of any kind is an intolerable interference with the right of the individual. He rebels at the oldfashioned idea of *loco parentis* and claims he is there to impart knowledge, not to substitute for absentee parents. But he can not escape a responsibility for the students' development of character and maturity.

Strangely and illogically, this is very often the same educator who interprets his academic freedom as the right to indoctrinate students with his view of things. Woe to the student who challenges his interpretation of history, or who questions the economic theory given as proven formula in what is, at best, a very inexact science. One thing we should all be agreed on is the university's obligation to teach, not indoctrinate.

Institutions of higher education are repositories of all the accumulated knowledge of man, but they must not be vending machines. Along with the dispensing of facts and figures must come the production of wisdom.

In our colleges today are undoubtedly more than one President of the United States, a number of supreme court justices, cabinet members, and many legislators.

And this brings me to the part higher education plays in contemporary America.

These institutions were created, and are presently maintained, to insure perpetuation of a social structure —a nation, if you will.

Now don't put a narrow intepretation on this as some will, and translate "social structure" into "status quo" or "social order" or "preserve the aristocracy; keep the little bananas from becoming top banana."

Our country, unfortunately, has a lot of people who would turn the country back to the dark ages, or ahead to 1984. Some have a concept of government more akin to Frederick the Great than Thomas Jefferson.

Our nation is founded on a concern for the individual and his right to fulfillment, and this should be the preoccupation of our schools and colleges. The graduate should go forth, literally starting on a lifetime of learning and growing and creativity that will in turn bring growth and innovation to our society.

And the truth is—never in history has there been such a need for men and women of wisdom and courage —wisdom to absorb the knowledge of the past and plan its application to the present and future, and courage to make the hard decisions.

At Stanford University in 1906 William James said, "The wealth of a nation consists more than in anything else in the number of superior men that it harbors."

At the risk of great oversimplification may I suggest that the great ideological split dividing us on the world scene and here within our own borders has to do with the place of the individual.

Acceptance is given more and more to the concept of lifting men by mass movements and collective action, in spite of the fact that history is strangely barren of any record of advances made in this manner. By contrast, the road from the swamp to the stars is studded with the names of individuals who achieved fulfillment and lifted mankind another rung.

It is time we realized what we mean by "equality" and being "born equal."

We are equal before God and the law, and our society guarantees that no acquisition of property during our lifetime, nor achievement, no matter how exemplary, should give us more protection than those of less prestige, nor should it exempt us from any of the restrictions and punishments imposed by law.

But let there be no misunderstanding about the right of man to achieve above the capacity of his fellows. The world is richer because of a Shakespeare and a Tennyson, a Beethoven and a Brahms. Certainly major league baseball would not be improved by letting every citizen have a turn at playing Willie Mays' position.

We live (even many so-called poor) at a level above the wildest dreams of the kings of one hundred years ago—because some individual thought of a horseless carriage, an ice box and later a refrigerator, or machinery that lifted burdens from our backs. (I would have thrown in television if I were still appearing on "Death Valley Days.") Why did so much of this develop so far and fast in America? Other countries are blessed with natural resources and equable climate—yes, and energetic and talented people. But here, to a degree unequalled any place in the world, we unleashed the individual genius of man, recognized his inherent dignity, and rewarded him commensurate with his ability and achievement.

Your generation is being wooed by many who charge this way we have known is inadequate to meet the challenges of our times. They point to the unsolved problems of poverty and prejudice as proof of the system's failure. As students, you have a duty to research to find if the failure is one of system—or is it the inadequacy of human nature?

You should also inquire if those who would replace the system have anything to offer in exchange other than untried theory packaged as Utopia. It sometimes seems strange that what is so often described as the brave new world of the future must be upheld by the collectivist philosophy of nineteenth-century theorists like Rousseau, Fourier, and Marx.

You have lived your entire lives in a governmental framework tending ever more toward the welfare state and centralism. We still have government of the people, by the people, and for the people, but there seems to be a lot more of "for" the people and less "of" and "by." This is justified on the claim that society has grown so complex we can no longer afford too much individual freedom.

To invoke "states' rights" is to be suspect of wanting to deny "human rights," and similar charges of selfishness greet *any* attack on the tendency of government to grow, but more particularly when attention is called to failures by government in the field of human welfare.

But you are students and therefore engaged in a search for truth.

Has the idea of a federation of sovereign states been proven unworkable because here and there selfish individuals used state government to impose on the freedom of some? Isn't there something to be said for a system wherein people can vote with their feet if government becomes too oppressive? Let a state pile on taxes beyond a bearable limit and business and industry start moving out and the people follow.

Let us think very carefully before switching to a system in which these states become administrative districts enforcing uniform laws and regulations.

If I may personalize here, let me tell you some of

what we have learned in California these past nine months. California—that is where they give governors on-the-job training. Being totally inexperienced, I had not learned all the things you cannot do, so I set out to keep my campaign promises. And once the people got over their shock they sort of took to the idea.

By every rule of reason, government "of" and "by" the people must be superior to any other kind. No government could possibly muster a group capable of making the multitudinous decisions that must be made every day to keep a society like ours moving.

If a state is to be great it must call upon the greatness of the people. And the people must be prepared to give a portion of their time to public affairs because government is their business. The only alternative to the people running government is government running the people.

We put together a blue-ribbon citizens committee to recruit personnel for the administrative posts that had to be filled by appointment. They did not just screen applicants for public jobs; they persuaded top level people in business and the professions to take jobs which represented tremendous personal sacrifce in salary in almost every case.

Then we invited the most successful citizens of our state to lunch and locked the doors. We outlined a plan for bringing their knowledge to bear on government. They were asked to give up their own careers for a period of from four to six months, to work full-time as members of task forces going into every agency and department of government to see how government could be made more efficient and economical by the use of modern business practices. And we asked them to put up the $250,000 it would take for administrative overhead in this undertaking.

They volunteered to a man, and they have just completed more than six months full-time away from their own pursuits and even their families. We are correlating their reports and putting their recommendations into operation. They range from methods of buying supplies to data-processing, from rotating department heads to consolidating files.

By applying the floor space standards of private industry to our own office employees, we will reduce this year our need for office space by two million square feet. We have already cancelled construction of a four million dollar building.

On their recommendations our phone bill will be reduced by two million dollars a year. Our budget for out-of-state travel by state employees has been cut 78 per cent and we have reduced the number of employees by 2½ per cent without a layoff or firing. We simply stopped hiring replacements for those who resigned or retired. Until this year the number of state employees had gone up each of the last eight years anywhere from 4 to 5½ per cent.

We have embarked on something we call the "Creative Society." It is nothing more than a full-time effort to involve the independent sector in finding and solving problems before government comes rushing in with bureaus that always seem to multiply like wire coat hangers in a closet.

Already we have thousands of industries—2,600 in Los Angeles, 1,500 in San Francisco, and so on throughout the state—organized and working in cooperation with our state employment service to match the hard-core unemployed in our poverty-pockets with jobs they can do or can be trained to do. The man in charge is working for no salary, and the cost of the program is borne by the industries.

Contrast this with the proposed poverty program I vetoed several weeks ago. It, too, was aimed at the hard-core unemployed. It was going to put seventeen of them to work clearing park land, but half the funds went for seven administrators to oversee the seventeen unemployed.

We need you—but we need *you* not just with a head full of packaged information marching in the ranks. We need you asking why, if we are so prosperous, should the numbers of those on welfare increase each year? Shouldn't welfare, if it is successful, be reducing the need for itself? Will we consider it a success when all of us are on public subsistence or should we judge its success on how many people it rescues *from* the dole?

We need answers to crime and why it has reached a critical point. Just blaming it on poverty will not do, because in the poverty of the great depression crime was at its lowest level and now in prosperity it has reached its peak.

Higher education in contemporary America has a sacred obligation to instill attitudes toward growth and learning that will in turn shape society. You are here to find yourselves as individuals, to at least have a chance to realize your potential.

The world is full of people who believe men need masters. Our society was founded on a different premise, but continuation of this way of ours is not inevitable. It will persist only if we care enough. We must care too much to settle for a non-competitive mediocrity. Only the best that is in each of us will do.

If it has seemed that we have left your generation with no cause to believe in, no banner to follow—you do have a cause here in this land. For one tick of history's clock we gave the world a shining golden hope. Mankind looked to us. Now the door is closing on that hope, and it could be your destiny to keep it open.

RONALD REAGAN

where. Our natural confidence about the future obscures awareness of how fragile it is. In this sense, we are isolating and alienating ourselves from the rest of the world as it really is.

In my talk today, I first want to take a quick look at the development problem—in terms of its size and national interest, and in terms of what needs to be done about it. Then, in more detail, I will discuss U. S. aid, trade, and private resources policies as they relate to development and suggest certain courses of action in these areas.

What are the dimensions of the development challenge?

The per capita gross national product of the United States is $3,240, its population 200 million. Mainland China's per capita gross national product is $85, its population 700 million. The per capita gross national product of West Germany is $1,620 and of Nigeria $80— both have a population of around 60 million. Japan and Indonesia are at roughly the same population level, but Japan is nine times better in productivity. Canada has one quarter the population and almost ten times the per citizen productive capacity of Brazil.

By the end of this century, on the present basis, the per capita income of Americans will have risen by thirty times as much as the increase in most underdeveloped countries. The world's population may jump to well over six billion by the end of this century, with nearly five billion living in the world's impoverished regions. The annual birth rate per 1,000 people in the industrialized nations is 20. But in those countries which are already unable to feed their populations adequately it is 40 per thousand.

Underdevelopment is a single word that sums up illiteracy, poverty, hunger, disease, human misery. It breeds violence and anarchy. It presents a vacuum. Underdevelopment is a greater danger than Communist aggression. The Communists exploit underdevelopment to spread their power and influence. They have carefully prepared for this by spreading the falsehood that the prosperity of the "have" nations resulted from their exploitation of the "have not" nations. Furthermore, they have erected a barrier to effective development by misleading "have not" nations into believing imperialism through private economic investment is as threatening to their independence as imperialism through political domination.

We must successfully attack the basic economic development problems now, or face more Vietnams later. And the dollar cost of the investment for peace is nowhere near the dollar cost for war.

If we remain an affluent island surrounded by a sea of poverty, our whole way of life will be threatened. If the lot of the deprived peoples does not improve, and if their hopes for a better life wither, widespread violence directly affecting life in the United States would be increased. If we—and I include our industrialized colleagues on this continent, in Europe, and the few in Asia—become the exclusive rich minority we will be dangerously vulnerable to the massive majority of the poor.

Because, generally speaking, the color line matches the division between the rich nations and the poor

GEORGE ROMNEY
123

nations, the possibilities are frighteningly explosive. This huge underdeveloped majority would have practically nothing to lose in the struggle.

Development is necessary for peace and peace is necessary for development. Turmoil defeats progress —abroad, as well as at home. Violence perpetuates human misery by discouraging the systematic organization of resources needed to raise living standards. But fear of instability should not be an excuse to maintain the status quo, nor can or should the revolution of rising expectations be suppressed because of the danger of disorder. It is critical that change occur, radical change, and quickly. But supporting change does not mean fomenting violence. We must guide change into constructive rather than destructive channels.

The national self-interest of America is directly, irrevocably dependent on international development. Underdevelopment represents not only threat but opportunity. As former Treasury Secretary C. Douglas Dillon said, "It is not missiles that have made neighbors of distant countries. It is the trading system of the modern world. . . . Today's less developed nations are tomorrow's richest economic and political asset."

The continued growth of private economies depends on the expansion of international trade and markets. Prospering nations make better customers and markets than poor ones. And among prospering nations political and social problems generally have a better chance of being resolved before they develop into military problems.

From an investment and enterprise standpoint, development of the underdeveloped can be more profitable than investing in activities in areas already developed. Here then is opportunity. What can be done about underdevelopment?

At present, our national response is characterized by lower levels of foreign economic assistance, heightened threats of protectionism, and insignificant private enterprise involvement in the business of development. There is a general failure of vision, will and leadership.

The total gross national product of all the industrial nations is currently $1.5 trillion per year. Only 1 per cent of that in economic aid—public and private—to the underdeveloped nations would amount to $15 billion annually. That would be double the present level. The flow of long-term capital from the "haves" to the "have nots" has remained about the same since 1961 despite a rise in national income of the richer nations.

There is no question that the industrialized nations can afford to meet the current growth needs of the developing nations without hurting themselves—in fact they can benefit themselves. In the case of the United States, our gross national product for 200 million people has increased by more than $100 billion since 1960, as compared with less than $35 billion for the more than 2 billion people in the less-developed world.

We are slipping—the gap is growing—the danger is increasing. We must find a way to avert this potential disaster for the world. We must concentrate new energies to use the tremendous wealth and technological expertise of the affluent northern nations to help develop the poverty-stricken southern peoples.

Bringing sustained growth out of stagnation is a

plodding process at best. It can't happen overnight. It must be conceived in terms of a generation of sustained effort. This is no Marshall Plan exercise, to rebuild highly sophisticated industrial economies. The underdeveloped nations are starting from scratch. They face economic handicaps not found by the now developed nations during their development. Most "have not" nations have no political tradition and little sense of nationhood. They have little base to build on, no institutional infrastructure, no large body of educated or trained manpower.

We cannot succeed if we act alone. We must be the leader largely through example. We must not be arbitrary or impatient in our approach to the problem. Nor can we be exclusive or paternalistic. The cooperative resources of the industrialized nations should be committed to the task in a coordinated manner, and the recipient nations must effectively marshal their own resources and pull their own share from the beginning. Otherwise, there is no chance of success. Progress-sharing partnerships between the affluent industrial countries and the underdeveloped areas should be a paramount objective of American foreign policy. This demands changes in our aid, trade and private resource policies, and needs a broad program of international cooperation.

The U. S. has not been responsive enough concerning measures to improve the terms of trade of the poorer nations. The industrial countries generally must be willing to allow the underdeveloped nations to strengthen their earnings from commercial exports.

Private enterprise embodies the very genius of the

American economy and carries the contagious germ of freedom. The underdeveloped world must be exposed to the dynamic private enterprise systems of the Northern Hemisphere, and a substantial inflow of private investment must be made available. Even under the most optimistic predictions on trade reform and private resource inflow, it is unlikely that the underdeveloped nations can achieve their development goals without more foreign aid.

The foreign aid program has few friends. It has no political constituency in the United States. It has made some bad errors. It has been wasteful. It has not shown quick or certain progress. Many nations that have received our aid appear ungrateful, and worse still, even oppose our position on major international issues. Sometimes our aid appears to shore up dictators. At other times it fills the pockets of corrupt politicians. Our military assistance and arms sales sometimes seem to encourage recipient countries to war against one another.

It is easy to criticize our aid program. It needs reshaping and continuing vigilant examination. But it is very difficult to administer an aid program in this interdependent but anti-cooperative world of today. Even so, there are some "success" stories, such as Taiwan, Israel, and South Korea. There has been isolated progress. And it is difficult to argue that government aid is not needed, given the development needs only it can fulfill, given the effect it can have on improving the environment for the inflow of private capital, and given the important ways in which it can complement the desirable effect of trade in development progress.

I believe that the private sector must supply the

bulk of the resources needed to assist the underdeveloped countries in their growth. But I also believe that our foreign aid levels have been cut below the amounts required for the necessary input of public funds in meeting the development challenge. As a percentage of our gross national product, American foreign aid has plummeted to a level about one-half that maintained during the last years of the Eisenhower Administration. The development loans requested by the Administration for the current fiscal year amount to only 78 per cent of the $975 million appropriated in 1963. The current Administration has shown little real leadership in international development, and the foreign aid program shows it. The complaints from the White House on Congressional cuts have usually come after the fact.

In competing with other budget priorities, foreign economic assistance gets lip service and little else. Thus it is unduly vulnerable to Congressional attack, and unreasonably becomes the butt of other frustrations. Overseas, it is looked upon as uncertain and undependable.

In 1957, John Foster Dulles testified for the establishment of the Development Loan Fund, stressing that it would be devoted to "the capital needed to create economic environment in which private initiative can come into play." The next year, he supported the principle of development loans, technical assistance, and self-help as key parts of the mutual security program, asking: "Are we so poor that we cannot afford to pay for peace and security and to continue to cultivate in the world those concepts of national independence and human liberty for which our nation was founded?"

Public monies help to improve the climate, build the institutions, and train technicians necessary to permit private enterprise to function effectively. A private investor looks for a stable governmental system committed to private enterprise, an equitable tax structure, a reasonable system of export controls, an educational system that can produce skilled manpower, an adequate and reasonably cheap power supply, a reliable transportation system, and wider markets. The aid program, directly and indirectly, can help provide these assets.

Government aid has other programs which encourage private investment in the underdeveloped areas. Among the most important are the Investment Survey, Investment Insurance, and Investment Loan programs. The extended risk guarantee program is particularly valuable, and Congress should authorize a higher ceiling on guarantees outstanding than now exists to help get it really moving.

Technical assistance in the foreign aid program is essential for development. Capital alone can't do the job if you don't have trained men to manage your projects. New machinery will gather rust if the people are starving and don't know how to raise or procure sufficient food to feed themselves. Our foreign aid program offers technical training in a host of fields and fights the war on hunger by encouraging both local food production and family planning efforts.

The U. S. foreign aid program channels money into international institutions such as the World Bank and various multilateral arrangements. It encourages cooperative and coordinated development assistance from other industrialized nations through multilateral organizations such as the Organization for Economic Co-operation and Development and its Development Advisory Committee.

Our foreign aid program needs reform, such as in the arms supply and sales field. It needs even more stress on certain basic principles, such as self-help, political development, and selective assistance to those nations most able and willing to make progress. It must not be relied on too much. There are many problems and limitations in government-to-government aid; there is much that it should not and more that it cannot do. I believe that we must put more stress on trade and private investment than on aid. But we need aid. One is not a substitute for another. All are closely inter-related; each can be complementary and catalytic.

The importance of trade policies and patterns to the development opportunity has been tragically underrated. The consumeristic private enterprise principles which our society has so effectively vitalized must be applied throughout the interdependent world. The continued support of international trade and the liberalization of existing trade restrictions must be pursued with a dedication and a vigor which has been sadly lacking, particularly in the present Administration.

The Kennedy Round of tariff negotiations achieved agreements affecting about $40 billion in world trade. We gave tariff cuts on $7.5 to $8 billion of our industrial and agricultural imports, and obtained tariff reductions on about the same amount of U. S. exports. This was progress. Our general experience shows that reduced tariff barriers bring about increased export earnings. Trade restrictionism has been tried and found to be a failure. But the Kennedy Round didn't really address the development challenge, and the Administration's position in the trade field as it pertains more directly to the poorer nations is uncertain and uncommitted.

The underdeveloped countries do not export many manufactured goods. Their raw material exports grow very slowly, whereas the demand for imported manufactured and industrial goods grows very quickly. There is a trade imbalance. In this situation, they lack the resources necessary to import the goods required to bring them to a satisfactory rate of development. So it is vital for the underdeveloped nations to trade more if they are to develop. And it is vital for the international community to create a trade environment that would foster rather than frustrate the growth of developing countries.

This is the basic aim of the United Nations Conference on Trade and Development, which meets again in New Delhi, India, in February. UNCTAD, as it is called, recommended in 1963 that the industrial countries extend general tariff preferences to imports from the underdeveloped countries in order to create markets for their manufactured exports and to bring about gradually the diminution of the obstacles hindering the entry of these exports to the industrial countries.

This move would improve the deteriorating terms of trade of the underdeveloped nations that I have mentioned. Allowing the poor nations to export more would enable them to import more, thus adjusting their trade imbalance and allowing them to get investment capital and capital equipment—crucially needed to achieve growth and stimulate development. This is a serious proposition, requiring careful study and consideration. In my view, given the priorities of the development challenge, America should support it. Instead, we have lacked the resolve. At the 1963 UNCTAD session, the U. S. opposed the proposal. I hope that our delegation to the next UNCTAD meeting will carry instructions allowing it to strongly support the general preference for the poorer nations in concert with a similar position by the other industrialized nations, as recently recommended by the OECD.

Extension of preferences by the U. S. to the underdeveloped nations would provide positive incentive to develop export trade. Preferences appear to be almost indispensable to the U. S. objective of increasing international trade and integrating the underdeveloped countries with the free economies of the North.

Recently, a huge upsurge of protectionist activity in the Congress—a retrogression into narrow economic nationalism—has raised the fears of many traders at home and abroad and cast new doubts on the basic underpinnings of our international economic relationships. The new, deadly serious, protectionist drive could affect 80 per cent of our dutiable imports. At one point, pending quota bills in Congress would have resulted in the drastic cutting back or cutting out of U. S. imports conservatively valued at $3.6 billion.

Now, the only answer to all this can be retaliation. According to the international system of trade rules under which we operate—the General Agreement on Tariffs and Trade—for every restriction we impose on imports, an equivalent restriction on our exports abroad can be imposed by other countries on U. S. industry. And retaliation to trade protectionism can also take the form of investment protectionism. If we want to sell, we must buy. When we try to insulate some sector of our industry from international competition, some U. S. business must in turn pay for it. And our overall, long-term trade position is hurt.

Retaliation to threatened protectionist moves could affect nearly one-third of our exports which face duties overseas. In addition, the quotas recommended would result in higher prices for U. S. consumers, worsen our critical balance of payments position, and increase Government controls over our own economy. The real problem is to correct the inflationary forces that are making us non-competitive and to encourage the forces that keep us ahead in productivity and technology.

The selfishness and short-sightedness of the protectionist movement is always beneath the surface. But I submit that a lack of dedication to the principles of international private enterprise and a lack of follow-up to the Kennedy Round achievements by the Johnson Administration actually encouraged this latest spate of restrictive threats. The present Administration even at this date has failed to present a bill to the Congress which would fill crucial gaps in our national trade policy. This legislation is needed, among other things, to restore the U. S. Government's unused negotiating authority which ran out on June 30, leaving us without the power to negotiate even minor tariff adjustments.

The new legislation must also liberalize the criteria for adjustment assistance under the 1962 Trade Expansion Act, which have proved in practice to be too tight and rigid for companies or industries in trouble. This unworkability of the adjustment help theoretically available to U. S. firms and workers injured by imports resulting from tariff concessions became clear many months ago. But nothing has been done by the Administration to remedy the situation. This inaction provided stimulus to the new protectionist wave. The Administration is tardy and unresolved in its trade policy and accordingly has courted confusion and reaction.

The greatest lack in the development effort today is the astounding absence of substantial participation by the private portion of our economy. Without the tremendous capital resources, the unparalleled know-how and the aggressive spirit of private enterprise, there is no possibility that the development gap can be effectively narrowed.

The present low rate of American investment represents a crippling failure of our own response to the development challenge. The private flow has been decreasing in terms of both gross national product and overall investment by the other northern industrialized nations. The total accumulated American private capital in the less developed countries today is only about $15 billion, over half of which is in extractive industries like mining and petroleum.

Given the great need of the poor nations for capital, the limitations on the amount and the efficiency of public funds, and the free enterprise traditions of this country, government aid should be a supplement to private involvement. At present the public commitment of funds is over four times the private commitment. The ratio is the opposite of what it should be. This is strange testimony to our own faith in private development.

What can be done about this private enterprise gap?

Ways must be found to diminish risk of loss and enhance the prospect of profit for the investor in the underdeveloped areas. Government policies should be revised to offer incentives to greater private involvement. Governments must cooperate on efforts to improve the private enterprise climate in the underdeveloped countries to attract both foreign and domestic investment.

Private business must perceive its own interests in broader and longer-range terms. The ultimate threat and opportunity must be clearly understood and accepted as a basis for action. The ingenuity of private enterprise must be devoted to applying the principles of progress-sharing and partnership in relations with foreign peoples, to put an end to fears of international economic imperialism and exploitation.

Private investment abroad must be viewed not just as a migration of capital but as a transfer of skills, knowhow, and techniques. The whole infrastructure of the private sector—management, sales, research and development, production—must be injected into the process.

Universities, foundations, and voluntary organizations must be brought into participation in the international development challenge on a more intensive and less peripheral scale than at present.

Representatives of business, finance, and industry from the various richer nations should consult and collaborate on private investments in the poorer countries.

There are instances of good recommendations and

good innovations in the area of private resource participation abroad. Let me give some examples.

The Report of the Advisory Committee on Private
Enterprise in Foreign Aid, submitted in 1965, and headed
by Arthur K. Watson, Chairman of the IBM World
Trade Corporation, contained some helpful suggestions,
many of which have been put into practice. Among
other proposals, the Watson Committee recommended
amendments in the tax law so that losses suffered by
American-owned subsidiaries in developing countries
could be offset against profits earned elsewhere. It also
recommended the less cautious use of the Agency for
International Development's extended risk guarantee
program, the subsidization of technical assistance to
institutions in the developing countries, and the expansion of AID's staff of private professionals in Washington and the field. It suggested that development be
given priority over immediate balance of payments con-
siderations and that special attention be given to the
role of agriculture in less-developed countries.

In activities abroad, U. S. firms have shown increasing interest in basic economic development projects, in
joint venture arrangements which help to foster the
concept of partnership, and in local management and
transfer to majority ownership.

The World Bank is investigating a multilateral investment guarantee formula which would expand the
concept of risk-reducing insurance on investments to a
shared arrangement involving the participation of the
recipient government. I have suggested an International Partnership Investment Insurance plan which
would provide a multilateral pool of private funds al-

lowing a radical expansion of the insurance principle.

Obstacle-free international trade bridges on a company-to-company or industry-to-industry basis have been constructed, such as in the agricultural implement and automotive industries of the United States and Canada.

The ADELA Investment Company—a multinational private investment group representing over 130 banks and industrial corporations of Canada, Western Europe, the U. S. and Japan—is hard at work mobilizing equity capital, know-how, and services for promising local, development-oriented enterprises in Latin America.

These ideas and activities are heartening, but they should be vastly expanded and multiplied. Others should be encouraged.

In the Executive Branch, I would recommend: reforms in the aid program and liberalization of southern trade, as I have indicated; greater diplomatic efforts to create better climates for private investment and more co-participation of industrialized nations in the development effort; increased tax incentives for foreign investment in the underdeveloped areas; beefing-up of existing investment guarantee programs; the enlargement at home and at posts abroad of the excellent activities of AID's Office of Private Resources; and stronger cross-governmental authority and action on policies affecting the less-developed areas such as the politics-ridden, bureaucracy-mired War on Hunger.

In the Congress, I would recommend the establishment of a Joint Congressional Committee on Private Initiative in International Development. Such an agency could enable the Congress to play a stronger and less parochial role in supporting the involvement of private enterprise in meeting the world-wide challenge, and would lend more prestige to the effort as a whole.

In the private sector itself, I would recommend the establishment of an International Development Coalition made up of representatives of business, finance, and industry, who would make continuing studies and recommendations to the private organizations on the one hand and to the Federal Government on the other concerning the best methods of private international investment and enterprise, and the best policies to facilitate such involvement.

CONTRIBUTORS

NORMAN COUSINS, Editor, *Saturday Review*
Address delivered April 4, 1967

J. W. FULBRIGHT, United States Senator from Arkansas
Address delivered May 5, 1967

ROBERT F. KENNEDY, United States Senator from New York
Address delivered March 18, 1968

MARTIN LUTHER KING, JR., President, Southern Christian
Leadership Conference
Address delivered January 19, 1968

ALFRED M. LANDON, Republican Presidential Candidate of 1936
Address delivered December 13, 1966

RALPH McGILL, Publisher, *The Atlanta Constitution*
Address delivered May 17, 1967

RONALD REAGAN, Governor of California
Address delivered October 26, 1967

GEORGE ROMNEY, Governor of Michigan
Address delivered December 6, 1967

This book was designed by Fritz Reiber. The text was set in 12/14 Caledonia, headings in Optima. It was printed on Perkins and Squier Wove 60-lb. Eggshell by the State Printer, Topeka, Kansas. The cover material is 10-pt. Kromekote white, bound at the State Bindery.

PRINTED BY
ROBERT R. (BOB) SANDERS, STATE PRINTER
TOPEKA, KANSAS
1968

32-2665